Praise for Michael E. Gerber, John K. Rost, and *The E-Myth Insurance Store*

I became a franchisee with Fiesta Auto Insurance in November 2008. This was when the world seemed to be falling apart and the beginning of a recession. I followed what Michael and John explain in their book and the franchise system. Now after four years my small investment in one store has turned into eleven successful franchise locations. I was working selling cell phones and now I am in charge of my destiny. This book and your hard work can make it happen for you too.

Oscar Neri, Fiesta Auto Insurance franchisee with 11 locations

This book underlines the important difference in leadership and management. Michael Gerber and John Rost go to great lengths and outline how Entrepreneurs get lost in their day-to-day operations. Entrepreneurs fail to see the importance of the big picture; developing a strategy to drive growth. Michael and John have a way to break down tactical systems and turn them into strategic thinking. This book is a must read for any entrepreneur; not only in this vertical market, but storefront operations too.

Dr. Mike Rodriguez, ABD, Organizational Leadership; Business Owner, Entrepreneur

The authors have taken what would otherwise be a dry discussion on motivating insurance agents, have applied the "E-Myth" magic, and have come up with an attainable roadmap to success for insurance and other service business entrepreneurs. A must read for every service professional!

Barry Kurtz Certified Specialist, Franchise & Distribution Law
The State Bar of California Board of Legal Specialization

Michael Gerber's *The E-Myth* is one of only four books I recommend as required reading. **For those looking to start and build a business of their own, this is the man who has coached more successful entrepreneurs than the next ten gurus combined.**

Everyone needs a mentor, someone who tells it like it is, holds you accountable, and shows you your good, bad, and ugly. For millions of small business owners, Michael Gerber is that person. Let Michael be your mentor and you are in for a kick in the pants, the ride of a lifetime.

Michael Gerber is a master instructor and a leader's leader. As a combat F15 fighter pilot, I had to navigate complex missions with life-and-death consequences, but until I read The E-Myth and met Michael Gerber, my transition to the world of small business was a nightmare with no real flight plan. **The hands-on, practical magic of Michael's turnkey systems magnified by the raw power of his keen insight and wisdom have changed my life forever.**

Michael Gerber's strategies in *The E-Myth* were instrumental in building my company from two employees to a global organization; I can't wait to see how applying the strategies from *Awakening the Entrepreneur Within* will affect its growth!

Michael Gerber's gift to isolate the issues and present simple, direct, business-changing solutions shines bright with *Awakening the Entrepreneur Within*. **If you're interested in developing an entrepreneurial vision and plan that inspires others to action, buy this book, read it, and apply the processes Gerber brilliantly defines.**

Michael Gerber truly, truly understands what it takes to be a successful practicing entrepreneur and business owner. He has demonstrated to me over six years of working with him that for those who stay the course and learn much more than just "how to work on their business and not in it" then they will reap rich rewards. **I finally franchised my business, and the key to unlocking this kind of potential in any business is the teachings of Michael's work.**

Chris Owen, marketing director, Royal Armouries (International) PLC

Michael's work has been an inspiration to us. His books have helped us get free from the out-of-control life that we once had. His no-nonsense approach kept us focused on our ultimate aim rather than day-to-day stresses. He has helped take our business to levels we couldn't have imagined possible. In the Dreaming Room made us totally re-evaluate how we thought about our business and our life. We have now redesigned our life so we can manifest the dreams we unearthed in Michael's Dreaming Room.

Jo and Steve Davison, founders, The Spinal Health Clinic
Chiropractic Group and www.your-dream-life.com

Because of Michael Gerber, I transformed my twenty-four-hour-a-day, seven-day-a-week job (also called a small business) into a multimillion turnkey business. This in turn set the foundation for my worldwide training firm. **I am living my dream because of Michael Gerber.**

Howard Partridge, Phenomenal Products Inc.

Michael Gerber is an outrageous revolutionary who is changing the way the world does business. **He dares you to commit to your grandest dreams and then shows you how to make the impossible a reality. If you let him, this man will change your life.**

Fiona Fallon, founder, Divine and The Bottom Line

Michael Gerber is a genius. Every successful business person I meet has read Michael Gerber, refers to Michael Gerber, and lives by his words. You just can't get enough of Michael Gerber. **He has the innate (and rare) ability to tap into one's soul, look deeply, and tell you what you need to hear. And then, he inspires you, equips you with the tools to get it done.**

Pauline O'Malley, CEO, TheRevenueBuilder

When asked "Who was the most influential person in your life?" I am one of the thousands who don't hesitate to say "Michael E. Gerber." **Michael helped transform me from someone dreaming of retirement to someone dreaming of working until age one hundred.** This awakening is the predictable outcome of anyone reading Michael's new book.

Thomas O. Bardeen

Michael Gerber is an incredible business philosopher, guru, perhaps even a seer. He has an amazing intuition, which allows him to see in an instant what everybody else is missing; he sees opportunity everywhere. **While in the Dreaming Room, Michael gave me the gift of seeing through the eyes of an awakened entrepreneur, and instantly my business changed from a regional success to serving clients on four continents.**

Keith G. Schiehl, president,
Rent-a-Geek Computer Services

Michael Gerber is among the very few who truly understand entrepreneur-ship and small business. While others talk about these topics in the form of theories, methodologies, processes, and so on, Michael goes to the heart of the issues. Whenever Michael writes about entrepreneurship, soak it in as it is not only good for your business, but great for your soul. His words will help you to keep your passion and balance while sailing through the uncertain sea of entrepreneurship.

Raymond Yeh, co-author, *The Art of Business*

Michael Gerber's insight, wisdom, caring, and straightforward approach helped me reinvent myself and my business while doubling my revenues in less than one year. Crack open this book and let him do the same for you, too.

Christine Kloser, author, *The Freedom Formula
and Conscious Entrepreneurs*

Michael Gerber forced me to think big, think real, and gave me the support network to make it happen. A new wave of entrepreneurs is rising, much in thanks to his amazing efforts and very practical approach to doing business.

Christian Kessner, founder, Higher Ground Retreats and Events

Michael's understanding of entrepreneurship and small business management has been a difference maker for countless businesses, including Infusion Software. **His insights into the entrepreneurial process of building a business are a must-read for every small business owner.** The vision, clarity, and leadership that came out of our Dreaming Room experience were just what our company needed to recognize our potential and motivate the whole company to achieve it.

Clate Mask, president and CEO, Infusion Software

Michael Gerber is a truly remarkable man. His steady openness of mind and ability to get to the deeper level continues to be an inspiration and encouragement to me. **He seems to always ask that one question that forces the new perspective to break open and he approaches the new coming method in a fearless way.**

Rabbi Levi Cunin, Chabad of Malibu

The Dreaming Room experience was literally life-changing for us. Within months, we were able to start our foundation and make several television appearances owing to his teachings. He has an incredible charisma, which is priceless, but above all Michael Gerber awakens passion from within, enabling you to take action with dramatic results. . . . starting today!

Shona and Shaun Carcary, Trinity Property Investments Inc. — Home Vestors franchises

I thought E-Myth was an awkward name! What could this book do for me? **But when I finally got to reading it . . . it was what I was looking for all along.** Then, to top it off, I took a twenty-seven-hour trip to San Diego just to attend the Dreaming Room, where Michael touched my heart, my mind, and my soul.

Helmi Natto, president, Eye 2 Eye Optics, Saudi Arabia

I attended In the Dreaming Room and was challenged by Michael Gerber to "Go out and do what's impossible." So I did; **I became an author and international speaker and used Michael's principles to create a world-class company that will change and save lives all over the world.**

Dr. Don Kennedy, MBA; author, *5 AM & Already Behind*, www.bahbits.com

I went to the Dreaming Room to have Michael Gerber fix my business. He talked about Dreaming. What was this Dreaming? I was too busy working! Too busy being miserable, angry, frustrated, behind in what I was trying to accomplish. And losing everything I was working for. **Then Michael Gerber woke up the dreamer in me and remade my life and my business.**

Pat Doorn, president, Mountain View Electric Ltd.

Michael Gerber can captivate a room full of entrepreneurs and take them to a place where they can focus on the essentials that are the underpinning of every successful business. He gently leads them from where they are to where they need to be in order to change the world.

Francine Hardaway, CEO, Stealthmode Partners;
founder, the Arizona Entrepreneurship Conferences

The E Myth

Insurance Store

*Why Most Insurance
Businesses Don't Work
and What to Do About It*

MICHAEL E. GERBER

JOHN K. ROST

PRODIGY
BUSINESS BOOKS

Published by
Prodigy Business Books, Inc., Carlsbad, California.

Production Team
Patricia Beaulieu, COO, Prodigy Business Books, Inc.; Steve Gottry, editor;
Erich Broesel, cover designer, BroeselDesign, Inc.; Nancy Ratkiewich, book production,
njr productions; Jeff Kassebaum, Michael E. Gerber author photographer, Jeff Kassebaum
and Co.; Sheri Geoffreys, John K. Rost author photographer.

For general information on other products and services, please visit the website:
www.michaelegerber.com.

ISBN 978-1-61835-008-4 (cloth)
ISBN 978-1-61835-010-7 (audio)
ISBN 978-1-61835-012-1 (ebk)

Printed in the United States of America

10 9 8 7 6 5 4 3 2 1

To Luz Delia, whose heart expands mine,
whose soul inspires mine,
whose boldness reaches for the stars, thank you,
forever, for being, truly mine…

—Michael E. Gerber

CONTENTS

A WORD ABOUT THIS BOOK

Michael E. Gerber

My first E-Myth book was published in 1985. It was called *The E-Myth: Why Most Small Businesses Don't Work and What To Do About It*.

Since I wrote that book and created a company to provide business development services to its many readers, millions have read *The E-Myth* and the book that followed it, called *The E-Myth Revisited*. In addition, tens of thousands have participated in our E-Myth Mastery programs.

John Rost, the co-author of this book, *The E-Myth Insurance Store*, was one of those more than enthusiastic readers, and as a direct result of his enthusiasm, his insurance store business became one of those clients. Over the years, John also became a very close friend of mine.

This book is two things: first, it is the product of my life-long work conceiving, developing, and growing the E-Myth way into a business model that has been applied to every imaginable kind of company in the world; second, it is a product of John's extraordinary experience and success applying the E-Myth to the development of his equally extraordinary business enterprise, Fiesta Auto Insurance.

So it was that one day, while sitting with my muse—which I think of as my inner voice and which many who know me think of as "here he goes again!"—I thought about the creation of an entire series of E-Myth vertical market books.

That series would be co-authored by experts in every industry who had successfully applied my E-Myth principles to the extreme development of a business—a very small company—with the intent of growing it nationwide or even worldwide. This is what John had in mind as he began to discover the almost infinite range of opportunities provided by thinking the E-Myth way.

Upon seeing the possibilities of this new idea, I immediately went to John and shared my excitement with him.

Not surprisingly, he said, "Let's do it!" And do it, we did.

Welcome to one of those many vertical market E-Myth expert books, *The E-Myth Insurance Store: Why Most Insurance Businesses Don't Work And What To Do About It.*

Read it, enjoy it, and let us—John and me—help you apply The E-Myth to the re- creation, development, and extreme growth of your entrepreneurial business into an enterprise that will make you justifiably proud.

To your life, your wisdom, and the life and success of your clients. Good reading!

—Michael E. Gerber
Co-Founder/Chairman
Michael E. Gerber Companies
Carlsbad, California
www.michaelegerber.com/co-author

A NOTE FROM JOHN

John K. Rost

The idea of sitting down one-on-one with individuals and selling insurance policies to them really doesn't appeal to me. So I don't do it. I used to do that, but I never will again. In fact, being completely transparent here, I don't even have a currently valid insurance license.

But the idea of helping people obtain affordable insurance that protects them and their families really *does* appeal to me. That's why I started my first insurance store and found competent, well-trained teammates to offer policies to our customers. That's also why I opened a second insurance store, and a third, and a fourth. Ultimately, that's also why I developed a plan to franchise my concept, Fiesta Auto Insurance, so that stores could be opened—and people's needs could be met—all across the United States.

The reality is that you do not have to become a Fiesta franchisee to become the successful owner-operator of an insurance store—or a group of insurance stores. All you need to do is apply the principles you'll discover in this book.

Insurance stores can be tailored to meet a variety of needs. In addition to offering affordable car insurance from a wide range of great providers, we also offer income tax preparation services through Fiesta Tax Service, available during "tax season" every year, right in our insurance store locations. You can do the same thing through your independent insurance-store operation. This book will teach you how to do exactly that!

This concept—and this ever-growing reality—didn't come about by accident. It is the result of the methodical application of Michael

Gerber's entrepreneurial principles, as espoused in *The E-Myth* and *The E-Myth Revisited*, as well as in his many other books. In this book, where E-Myth meets the insurance store, our goal is to open up unlimited opportunities for any entrepreneur who desires to serve the needs of others while building a better future for himself or herself.

Of course, to be successful in the insurance field, you don't have to become a Fiesta Auto Insurance franchisee. You can open your own store and apply the same basic principles to your insurance business. The E-Myth principles—and the principles of this book—are universal.

And, if you already have an established business—something I refer to as a "mom-and-pop" insurance store (and I do not mean that derogatorily in any way…I simply mean you have one store and you and possibly your spouse are the sole owners and operators)—I want to inspire you to look beyond your present business situation, and move forward toward greater opportunities.

At Fiesta, our motto—our business slogan—is "Dream, Believe, Achieve." That could easily be Michael Gerber's motto, too. Together, through this book, we hope to help you dream what may be a new, unexpected dream, believe in that dream to the point where you take action, and transform that action into great success.

Our goal is to help you discover a unique niche in which you can help others while enjoying a level of success you never imagined. Whether you decide to stake your future with Fiesta, with another company, or on your own, is irrelevant. We simply aim to give you the tools you need to succeed. By applying Michael's solid, proven E-Myth principles with the lessons I've learned along the way, we can virtually insure—I mean ensure—your success.

It's time to put E-Myth to work in your life and your business!

—John K. Rost
President
Fiesta Insurance Franchise Corporation
Huntington Beach, CA
www.FiestaFranchise.com

PREFACE

Michael E. Gerber

I am not in the insurance business, though I have helped count-less insurance agents and entrepreneurs reinvent their businesses over the past 35 years.

I like to think of myself as a thinker, maybe even a dreamer. Yes, I like to do things. But before I jump in and get my hands dirty, I prefer to think through what I'm going to do and figure out the best way to do it. I imagine the impossible, dream big, and then try to figure out how the impossible can become the possible. After that, it's about how to turn the possible into reality.

Over the years, I've made it my business to study how things work and how people work—specifically, how things and people work best together to produce optimal results. That means creating an organization that can do great things and achieve more than any other organization can. Or, in the case of the insurance business, a company that surpasses the competition and provides high standards of service, high income to its owner, and equally high job satisfaction to all who work there.

The end product of my efforts has been a series of books I've authored—*The E-Myth* books—as well as a company, E-Myth Worldwide, which I founded in 1977, and Chief Dreamer Enterprises, launched in 2005.

For over 30 years, my first company, E-Myth Worldwide, helped tens of thousands of small business owners, including many in the insurance field, reinvent the way they do business by (1) rethinking the purpose of their companies, and (2) imagining how they could fulfill their purpose in innovative ways.

Many business owners view day-to-day management as an unwelcome burden that distracts them from their main responsibility of meeting the needs of their clients, creating and closing transactions, and—not least of all—getting paid.

Yet business management—what I like to call *business liberation*—can be just as exciting (and lucrative) as selling a thousand policies to a thousand clients.

This book is about how to produce the best results as a real-world insurance entrepreneur in the development, expansion, and, yes, *liberation* of your career. In the process, you will come to understand what insurance—as a *business*—is and what it isn't.

This intentionally small book is about big ideas. The topics we'll be discussing here are the very issues that you face daily in your business venture—no matter what it is. You know what they are: People, Money, Management, and many more. My aim is to help you begin the exciting process of totally transforming the way you do business.

With that said, I'm confident that *The E-Myth Insurance Store* could well be the most important book in building your entrepreneurial venture as any you'll ever read.

Unlike other books on the market, my book won't tell you how to do the work you do. Instead, my goal is to share with you the E-Myth philosophy as a way to revolutionize the way you *think* about the work you do. I'm convinced that this new way of thinking is something entrepreneurs everywhere must adopt in order for their businesses to flourish during these trying times. I call it strategic thinking, as opposed to tactical thinking.

In strategic thinking—also called systems thinking—you will begin to think about your entire business—the broad scope of it—instead of focusing on its individual parts. You will begin to see the end game (perhaps for the first time) rather than just the day-to-day routine that's consuming you—the endless, draining work I call "doing it, doing it, doing it."

Understanding strategic thinking will enable you to create a business that becomes successful, with the potential to flourish as an even more successful enterprise. But in order for you to accomplish this, your business—and certainly your enterprise—must work *apart* from you, instead of *because* of you.

The E-Myth philosophy says that a good idea can grow into a highly successful business, which in turn can become the foundation for an inordinately successful enterprise that runs smoothly and efficiently *without* the owner having to be in the office for 12 hours a day, 6 or 7 days a week. As you will discover, that's exactly how my co-author, John Rost, operates his business, lives his dream, and *enjoys* his life.

So what is "The E-Myth," exactly? The E-Myth is short for the Entrepreneurial Myth, which says that most businesses fail to fulfill their potential because most people starting their own business are not entrepreneurs at all. They're actually what I call *technicians suffering from an entrepreneurial seizure.* When technicians suffering from an entrepreneurial seizure start a business of their own, they almost always end up working themselves into a frenzy, going straight from one day to the next and hardly ever taking a break. They're burning the candle at both ends, fueled by too much coffee and too little sleep, and most of the time, they can't even stop to think. If this sounds familiar, keep reading.

In short, The E-Myth says that most insurance entrepreneurs don't own a true business—most own a job disguised as a business. They're doing it, doing it, doing it, hoping like hell to get some time off, but never figuring out how to get their business to run without them. And if your business doesn't run well without you, what happens when you can't be in two places at once? Ultimately, your business will fail.

It's happening throughout the insurance world even as you're reading these words. In today's economy, fewer and fewer people are living the lives they had hoped to live when they first started their businesses, and more and more are failing.

The good news is that you don't have to be among the statistics of failure in the insurance field. The E-Myth philosophy I am about to share with you in this book has been successfully applied to tens of thousands of businesses just like yours with extraordinary results.

The key to transforming your business—and your life—is to grasp the profound difference between going to work *on* your insurance business (systems thinker) and going to work *in* your insurance business (tactical thinker). In other words, it's the difference between going to work *on* your business as an entrepreneur and going to work *in* your business as a salesperson.

The two are not mutually exclusive. In fact, they are essential to each other. The problem with most insurance businesses is that the systems thinker—the entrepreneur—is completely absent. And so is the vision.

The E-Myth philosophy says that the key to transforming your business into a successful enterprise is knowing how to transform yourself from a successful insurance technician (contract-writing agent) into a successful technician-manager-entrepreneur. In the process, everything you do in your business will be transformed. The door is then open to turning your company into the kind of enterprise it should be: a growing business, an enterprise of pure joy!

It's my thesis that The E-Myth not only *can* work for you, but that it *will* work for you. And in the process it will give you an entirely new experience of your business and beyond.

To your future and your life. Good reading.

—Michael E. Gerber
Co-Founder/Chairman
Michael E. Gerber Companies
Carlsbad, California
www.michaelegerber.com/co-author

ACKNOWLEDGMENTS

Michael E. Gerber

As always, and never to be forgotten, there are those who give of themselves to make my work possible.

To my dearest and most forgiving partner, wife, friend, and co-founder, Luz Delia Gerber, whose love and commitment takes me to places I would often not go unaccompanied.

To Steve Gottry, whose bright attitude, dogged determination, and love for the cause has consistently made our mission a reality, a big thank you.

To Erich Broesel, our stand-alone graphic designer and otherwise visual genius who supported the creation of all things visual that will forever be all things Gerber, we thank you, deeply, for your continuous contribution of things both temporal and eternal.

To Trish Beaulieu, wow, you are splendid.

And to Nancy Ratkiewich, whose work has been essential for you who are reading this.

To those many, many dreamers, thinkers, storytellers, and leaders, whose travels with me in The Dreaming Room have given me life, breath, and pleasure unanticipated before we met. To those many participants in my life (you know who you are), thank you for taking me seriously, and joining me in this exhilarating quest.

And, of course, to my co-authors, all of you, your genius, wisdom, intelligence, and wit have supplied me with a grand view of the world, which would never have been the same without you.

Love to all.

ACKNOWLEDGMENTS

John K. Rost

Every one of us needs people in our lives who believe in our dreams, support us, and love us unconditionally. For me, those special people have long been my three amazing teenage children—though they are hardly children any more.

My children have been the ones who suffered the most while I was building my businesses. They have had to put up with a stressed dad who often came home late and took endless business calls in the evening and on weekends. I am very proud of Alec, Christopher, and Emily. They are my awesome support team—they inspire me to succeed in every endeavor. I hope they are now enjoying the vacations and "free" college educations that have come about because their father owns a successful enterprise.

My Grandfather, Alfred Bell, and Grandmother, Dorris Bell, (both on my mother's side) who have long since passed, were tremendous motivators and mentors for me as an adolescent and young man. They always coached me and held me to very high standards that have helped me achieve many goals and inspire others around me. Their love, character-building efforts, financial support, and model of integrity define who I am today.

My loving sister, Suzanne, has always been a proud supporter of everything I've wanted to pursue in my life. I am equally proud of her achievements. She helps people who have mental and physical limitations, as the gifted CEO of her nonprofit group, Stand Together and Recover Centers (S.T.A.R.), based in the Phoenix, Arizona, metropolitan area. We thoroughly enjoy sharing our dreams and experiences with each other.

My appreciation and gratitude quickly extend to our Fiesta Auto Insurance franchisees. They were willing to follow a dream that I created—and, in many cases, had to risk their entire life savings to start and build successful franchises. Because we all trust one another, they have freely offered an enormous amount of feedback that continues to refine our systems and make it easier for new franchise owners to succeed.

My staff over the years has been nothing short of amazing! They demonstrate a level of loyalty and dedication that I've seldom witnessed in any business or organization. They are dedicated to me, to the company, and to our system—and they give so much of themselves to ensure that we grow and continue to become more successful with each exciting new year.

I need to acknowledge the team that has stood behind me to develop the content and message of this book. Steve Gottry, an accomplished author and fellow pilot, was committed from day one to help me bring my ideas to life on these pages. And Trish Beaulieu has gently yet firmly guided the entire process through both her administrative abilities and her editing skills.

Last, but certainly not least, I want to thank my friend and mentor, Michael Gerber, the "E-Myth Guru," for taking me on board to do this book. His wisdom has inspired me, his teachings have guided me, and his sense of humor has sustained me when I most needed it. Thank you, Michael!

INTRODUCTION

Michael E. Gerber

What do you really want out of life?

Do you want to start and operate a business that owns you? That owns your time? That swallows your money—your investment—without warning and without mercy? Do you want to discover the meaning of stress? Sleepless nights? The negative physical outcome of little or no exercise?

Or do you want to climb and conquer mountains in your life, either figuratively or in reality? Do you desire to "get acquainted" with your family again? Sleep peacefully? Enjoy a social life? AND do all this while growing your enterprise and your bank account?

The fact is, a successful insurance store owner works balanced hours, has little stress, is engaged in rich and rewarding relationships with friends and family, and has an economic life that is diverse, fulfilling, and shows a continuous return on investment.

A successful insurance entrepreneur finds time and ways to give back to the community, but at little cost to his or her sense of ease.

A successful insurance entrepreneur is a leader who has much more to do than teach clients how to protect their future (or, in the case of John's business, also help them save money on taxes). He or she has to be a leader, a strong father, mother, wife, or husband; a friend, teacher, mentor; a spiritually grounded human being; and a person who lives a life that not only *insures* other people, but also *assures* other people. This is the kind of person who builds others up and helps them reach their full potential.

I know what you're thinking. Sightings of successful people, thus defined, are approximately as rare as sightings of the Loch Ness Monster.

So let's go back to the original question: What do you really want out of life?

I don't know how you've answered that question in the past—or how you are answering it today—but I am confident that once you understand the strategic thinking laid out in this book, you will answer it differently in the future.

If the ideas here are going to be of value to you, it's critical that you begin to look at yourself in a different, more productive way. I am suggesting you go beyond the mere technical aspects of your daily job in insurance and begin instead to think strategically about your store as both a business and an enterprise.

I often say that most *businesses* don't work—the people who own them do. In other words, most insurance stores simply are jobs for the people who own them. Does this sound familiar? The agent, overcome by an entrepreneurial seizure, has started his or her own agency, become his or her own boss, and now works for a lunatic!

The result: they are running out of time, patience, and—ultimately—money. Not to mention paying the worst price anyone can pay for the inability to understand what a true business is, and what a true enterprise is—the price of his or her life.

In this book I'm going to make the case for why you should think differently about what you do and why you do it. It isn't just the future of your business that hangs in the balance. It's the future of your life.

The E-Myth Insurance Store is an exciting departure from my other sole-authored books. In this entire series of books directed to specific fields, E-Myth experts—professionals who have successfully applied the E-Myth to the development of their enterprises—are sharing their secrets about how they achieved extraordinary results using the E-Myth paradigm. In addition to the time-tested E-Myth strategies and systems I'll be sharing with you in this book, you'll benefit from the wisdom, guidance, and practical tips provided by a man whose insurance business works for him—rather than the other way around.

The problems that afflict insurance businesses today are the same problems confronting every organization of every size, in every industry in every country in the world. This series of E-Myth "expert books" in all major industries will serve as a way for Michael E. Gerber Partners™ to bring a legacy of expertise to the world of small, struggling businesses. The series will offer an exciting opportunity to understand and apply the significance of E-Myth methodology in both theory and practice to businesses in need of development and growth.

The E-Myth says that only by conducting your business in a truly innovative and independent way will you ever realize the unmatched joy that comes from creating a truly independent business; a business that works *without* you rather than *because* of you.

The E-Myth says that it is only by learning the difference between the work of a *business* and the business of *work* that entrepreneurs will be freed from the predictable and often overwhelming tyranny of the unprofitable, unproductive routine that consumes them on a daily basis.

The E-Myth says that what will make the ultimate difference between the success or failure of your insurance enterprise is first and foremost how you *think* about your business, as opposed to how hard you work in it.

So, let's think it through together. Let's think about those things—work, people, money, time—that dominate the world of entrepreneurs everywhere.

Let's think about planning. About growth. About management. About getting a life!

Let's think about improving you and your family's life through the development of an extraordinary business. About getting a life that's *yours.* ♣

The Story of Marcos and Teresa

Michael E. Gerber

You leave home to seek your fortune and, when you get it, you go home and share it with your family.

—*Anita Baker*

E very business is a family business. To ignore this truth is to court disaster. This is true whether or not family members actually work in the business.

Whatever their relationship with the business, every member of an entrepreneur's family will be greatly affected by the decisions he or she makes about the business.

Unfortunately, insurance agents tend to compartmentalize their lives unless some family members are actively involved in their business. They see their business as separate from their family, and therefore none of their family's business.

"This doesn't concern you," says one agent to her husband.

"I leave business at the office and my family at home," says another agent, with blind conviction.

And with equal conviction, I say, "Not true!"

In actuality, your family and your business are inextricably linked to one another. What's happening at the office is also happening at home. Consider the following and ask yourself if each is true:

- If you're angry at work, you're also angry at home.

- If you're out of control in your business, you're equally out of control at home.

- If you're having trouble with money in your business, you're also having trouble with money at home.

- If you have communication problems in your business, you're also having communication problems at home.

- If you don't trust in your business, you don't trust at home.

- If you're secretive in your business, you're equally secretive at home.

And you're paying a huge price for it!

The truth is that your business and your family are one—and you're the link. Or you should be. Because if you try to keep your work life and your family apart—if your business and your family are strangers—you will effectively create two separate worlds that can never wholeheartedly serve each other. Two worlds that split each other apart.

Let me tell you the story of Marcos and Teresa.

Marcos and Teresa met when he was in his first year of community college, pursuing an Associate's Degree in Bookkeeping. She was a senior in a nearby high school and had a part-time job at IHOP. Marcos liked to take a study break at IHOP, but from the first moment he saw Teresa, school was the last thing on his mind. She had long, dark, flowing hair, often tied back in a ponytail, she wore the hottest shade of lipstick he had ever seen, and she even looked good in that silly uniform.

Marcos said to himself, "I am going to date that girl." Being a "proper" person who was raised with an understanding of respect, he told Teresa of his intentions, but insisted on meeting her family first. Her dad loved that about him from the day they all met at her house.

When Teresa graduated from high school, she enrolled in the same two-year college with the goal of becoming a nurse. Marcos graduated at the end of her first year, and went on a long, dreary search for a job in a corporate accounting department. He found one at a small software development company. The pay was not what he had hoped, and his boss was a tyrant. But he stayed with it for more than a year, complaining about it to Teresa every time they were together.

"I have interviews at four hospitals and an emergency clinic in the next three weeks," she announced proudly. "When I get a job, that will give you the freedom to quit your job if you want and look for something that makes you happy."

"That's the perfect plan," Marcos agreed. "Except for one thing: I want to be married. Will you marry me, Teresa?"

While it wasn't quite the romantic proposal she had hoped for, she immediately and enthusiastically accepted. And off they went to see her dad. He immediately blessed the idea, as did Teresa's mom.

Teresa was hired immediately by a large hospital, and Marcos soon found what he thought was the perfect job—as an insurance agent for a "captive agency," which simply meant that he would be representing one insurance company, as opposed to working for an "independent agency," in which he would represent multiple insurance companies. He studied diligently for all the exams required by the government regulatory agencies and passed with ease.

Marcos was confident that, with his wife happily employed and his own major career decision behind him, this would be the perfect time to get married. She agreed, but it still took her seven months to plan the event. Weddings are no small events in her family's tradition.

"I love what I do," Marcos announced to his new bride over one of their frequent "Memory Lane" breakfasts at IHOP, "but I don't feel that I'm always serving my clients in the best way possible. I'm not giving them choices. The only options they have are the scope and amounts of coverage they take with my company. I can't help them shop for competitive rates with other companies."

"On the other hand," Teresa countered, "you're making fairly good money."

"I know. But my future is limited. I get a paycheck every two weeks, but it will never grow by much. The boss makes all the money. You know how that goes."

"So what do you want to do?" she asked gently.

"I've been looking into becoming an independent agent. You know, represent several companies so I can offer choices to my clients, rather than being captive to one company. I've done some research, and this seems easier than I originally thought it would be."

Marcos explained all the details to his wife, as best he understood them. She agreed this could be a good move. *Could* be. But in the backs of their minds, they both knew this new venture could involve great risk. Little did they know at the time how many challenges they would face.

One beautiful sunny day, Marcos walked out the door with an extra spring in his step. He drove the three miles to his brand new independent insurance agency, admired the sign above the entrance that simply read "Insurance," and hung an "OPEN" sign in the window for the very first time. He was in business!

His office was simple: one used metal desk with a new computer perched on top, a four-drawer file cabinet, a swivel chair and three chairs for visitors, a coffee table with stacks of old magazines he had scrounged, and a water cooler. There were signs on the walls that indicated which companies his new agency represented.

"Still smells like fresh paint," he said aloud, even though no one else was in the room. "Oh, well, that will fade away in a couple days."

He hadn't been there for more than a half hour when a young man, probably in his late twenties or early thirties, walked in.

"I just moved here from Michigan, and I need to get car insurance."

After determining his prospect's needs, Marcos explained the features, benefits, and costs of the policies offered by various underwriters.

"I don't have to be a farmer to buy that company's policy, do I?" the young man asked, completely innocently.

Though actually chuckling inside, Marcos kept his composure, smiled, and replied, "No, you don't."

In a matter of minutes, the policy was written, and the first client of the new insurance store drove away in his newly insured car.

Despite that "fast start," business was slow for quite a long time. Marcos hadn't really given any thought to marketing, and there was no one he could turn to for help. He eventually decided to try putting some signs in the window, including one that read "Se Habla Español." That didn't really help, because there were very few Hispanics living in the area near the store. Though fluent in Spanish himself, he attributed the lack of Spanish-speaking clients to his location.

For the first several months, Marcos was the only person in the office—no other staff members were needed. He brought his lunch, took very short breaks, and put in long hours, hoping that by being open late, he would draw more business. But, again, he had no one to help him figure all of this out.

Over time, mostly through trial and error, but also with a lot of ideas from his very creative wife, Marcos found the right combination of window signs that drew in more prospects. He actually started to make a profit—something he and Teresa celebrated with dinner out …at 9:00 p.m., after he finally got home.

It wasn't long before Marcos was in the financial position to add another agent, then an administrative assistant, and then another agent. He was no longer on his own; he had an actual growing business.

Of course, managing a business was more complicated and time-consuming than he had projected. He not only supervised his team, but he also was continually looking for ways to keep everyone busy and productive. He had to devise a training program so that his new team of today—and tomorrow—would all operate under the same systems, standards, and procedures. He had searched for some standardized programs, but there simply weren't any out there.

As the months went by and more and more clients (and team members) came through the door, Marcos had to spend even more time just trying to keep his head above water.

He began leaving home earlier in the morning and returning home later at night. He rarely saw his wife anymore. And when their daughter was born, he barely had any time to spend with her—and he always believed that being a dad would be a priority in his life. For the most part, Marcos was resigned to the problem. He saw the hard work as essential to building the "sweat equity" he had long heard about.

Money was also becoming a problem for Marcos. Although the business was growing like crazy, money always seemed scarce when it was really needed. Just when he thought he was in control of the situation, there would be a rash of policy cancellations. That really hurt, because he still had to deal with his ever-increasing overhead. No matter what factors impacted his cash flow, Marcos still had to pay his people, the rent, the phone bill, the Internet bill, and the insurance coverage for his business. This became a persistent problem. Marcos often felt like a juggler dancing on a tightrope. A fire burned in his stomach day and night.

To make matters worse, Marcos began to feel that Teresa was insensitive to his troubles. So he tried to avoid talking to his wife about the business. "Business is business" was Marcos's mantra. "It's my responsibility to handle things at the office and Teresa's responsibility to take care of our daughter, the house, and me."

Teresa's seeming lack of understanding rankled Marcos. Didn't she see that he had a growing business to take care of? That he was doing it all for her and their daughter? And the future? Apparently not.

As time went on, Marcos became even more consumed by his business. Not surprisingly, Teresa grew more frustrated by her husband's lack of communication and increasingly long hours. When the business had become more successful, she put her nursing career on hold to focus on their family. And now her husband was barely ever at home. Their relationship grew tense and strained. The rare moments they were together were more often than not peppered by long silences—a far cry from the impassioned dreaming that had characterized their relationship's early days.

Meanwhile, Rebecca, the administrative assistant, was becoming a problem for Marcos. Rebecca never seemed to have the financial information Marcos needed to make decisions about payroll, commissions pending, and general operating expenses, let alone how much profit could be projected.

When questioned, Rebecca would shift her gaze to her feet and say, "Listen, Marcos, I've got a lot more to do around here than you can imagine. It'll take a little more time. Just don't press me, okay?"

Overwhelmed by his own work, Marcos usually backed off. The last thing Marcos wanted was to upset Rebecca and have to do the books himself. He believed he had waved a permanent "good-bye" to that part of his past. He could empathize with what Rebecca was going through, given the growth of the business. But bookkeeping? "No, thank you!"

Late at night in his office, Marcos would sometimes recall his first years as a captive agent working for a large insurance company. He missed the simple life! Fewer responsibilities!

Then, as quickly as the thoughts came, they would vanish. He had work to do and no time for daydreaming. "Having my own business is a great thing," he would remind himself. "I simply have to apply myself and get on with the job. I have to work as hard as I always have when something needed to get done."

Marcos began to live most of his life inside his head. He began to distrust his people. They never seemed to work hard enough or to care about his agency as much as he did. If he wanted to get something done, he usually had to do it himself.

Then one day, Rebecca quit in a huff, frustrated by the amount of work that he was demanding of her. Marcos was left with a desk full of papers and a mountain of other problems that continued to grow. His world turned upside down.

Why had he been such a fool? Why hadn't he taken the time to learn what Rebecca contributed at the office? Why had he waited until now?

Ever the trouper, Marcos plowed into Rebecca's job with every shred of energy he could muster. What he found shocked him. Rebecca's workspace was a disaster area! Her desk drawers were a jumble of papers, coins, pens, pencils, erasers, rubber bands, envelopes, business cards, and candy.

"What was she thinking?" Marcos raged.

When he got home that night, even later than usual, he got into a shouting match with Teresa. He settled it by storming out of the house to get a drink. Didn't anybody understand him? Didn't anybody care what he was going through? Was there no justice in the world?

He returned home only when he was sure Teresa was asleep. As he walked by the computer, he noticed an unfinished email up on the screen. One phrase practically leapt off the page: "Do you know of any good divorce lawyers? Is there anyone at the firm where you work who could help me?"

The e-mail was from his wife to her sister.

That night Marcos slept on the couch. He left early in the morning before his wife and daughter were awake. He knew there was no way he could face them.

On his way to the office, Marcos stopped at a 24-hour liquor store and bought the largest bottle of tequila he could find…and you can imagine how the story goes from here.

What lessons can we draw from Marcos and Teresa's story? As I've already emphatically said, every business is a family business. Every business profoundly touches every family member, even those not working in the business. Every business either gives to the family or takes from the family, just as individual family members do.

If the business takes more than it gives, the family is always the first to pay the price.

In order for Marcos to free himself from the prison he had created, he would first have to admit his vulnerability. He would have to confess to himself and his family that he really didn't know enough about his own business, nor the secrets of how to grow it.

Marcos tried to do it all himself. Had he succeeded, had the business supported his family in the style he imagined, he would have burst with pride. Instead, he unwittingly isolated himself, thereby achieving the exact opposite of what he sought.

He destroyed his life—and his family's life along with it. Repeat after me: *Every business is a family business.*

Are you like Marcos? I believe that all entrepreneurs share a common soul with him. You must learn that a business is only a business. It is not your life. But it is also true that your business can have a profoundly negative impact on your life unless you learn how to do it differently than most people do it. Differently than Marcos did it.

Marcos' insurance agency could have served his and his family's life. But for that to happen, he would have had to learn how to master his venture in a way that was completely foreign to him.

Instead, Marcos' business consumed him. Lacking a true understanding of the essential strategic thinking that would have allowed him to create something unique, Marcos and his family were doomed before he even opened his doors.

This book contains the secrets that Marcos should have known. By applying the principles we'll discuss here, you can avoid a similar fate.

Let's start with the subject of *money*. But, before we do, let's listen to John's views on the story I just told you. ❖

What Do You Really Want? Envision It!

John K. Rost

The only thing that will stop you from fulfilling your dreams is you.
—Tom Bradley

I believe that it's normal and natural for all of us to have dreams. We dream of a better life…a successful life…a rewarding life. We imagine a happy spouse, amazing children, plentiful money, and toys that we can enjoy on long weekends. A boat, maybe. A cabin in the woods. A pair of Harleys. A vacation in Hawaii. Yes, that all happens for some people in the world. But not for all of us.

That's because I also believe that the world is made up of three kinds of people: Successes, Failures, and those who *should* be successes, but somehow just "missed it by that much." (For those of you who remember the old TV hit, *GET SMART*, that phrase just might resonate!)

It seems to me that few things go wrong in the lives of Successes. They appear to be born to succeed. They have the Midas touch. Every idea, every investment, every venture turns to gold. However, I don't know any of these people. I've heard they're out there somewhere, but I've never met them.

Then there are the Failures. Poor, sad, disillusioned people. Everything they touch turns to cow chips. (If you don't know what I mean by that term, *Google* it!) Every idea, every investment, every venture instantly transforms into, well...cow chips. But I don't know any of these people, either. I'm sure they exist, but I've never met them.

Finally, there are the people who have "missed it by that much." These are the men and women who have some good ideas, make some sound investments, and make some money on their ventures. Or not. Yes...or no. In other words, it's all hit or miss. I know lots of these people. I've met them; I've talked to them face-to-face. I'm happy for those who get a "hit," and I grieve with those who somehow miss.

Michael's goal, since he first wrote *The E-Myth*—and followed it later with other equally helpful, inspiring, insightful books—is to help his millions of readers, possibly you among them, avoid missing it by that much. Michael understands, better than anyone I know, that a successful business enterprise is not an accident. It's the result of a plan.

Our shared goal is to help our readers become successes as owners/operators of growing insurance stores.

Throughout the process of growing my insurance enterprise, I have observed that the people who understand and apply E-Myth principles in their businesses—whether fledgling or well-established—are, more likely than not, able to avoid "missing it by that much."

Many people I know create what's known as a Vision Board. It may be on their computers, or it may be an actual stand-up cardboard poster that they look at every day when they get up in the morning, as well as before they go to bed at night.

No matter what is on your Vision Board, one essential component should be a picture of your family. After all, that is likely why you're doing what you're doing. And, as Michael says, "Every business is a family business."

In your case, your family may not directly be a part of your insurance store. They may not go to work with you every day and lock the door and drive home with you at night. They may not be a part of your *operations*. But they *must* be a part of your *dream*. Your spouse, your kids, and even your extended family and your in-laws should be a part of your support team. They need to realize that there will be times when you will get home later than usual; or times when you have to leave for work before breakfast; or times when you will have to bring home paperwork (and its accompanying stress) and work late into the night. There will be times when, sadly, you will have to miss games and recitals and other events. (Do your best not to miss birthdays, though!)

You want the rest of the family to understand what's going on and be, in a sense, working together with you, instead of working against your dream.

To bring them all into sync with your business objectives, you must draw them in. You must tell them what you are doing, why you are doing it, and what you see as the future of your business.

Your Vision Board can help. I know insurance store owners who will attach pictures of a boat or an RV or a particular vacation destination to their vision boards. They might even include a graph that indicates how far along they are in reaching their goals.

I know owners who began with pictures of a small fishing boat, or a pop-up tent trailer, or Space Mountain at Disneyland, and after they reached those goals, they replaced those pictures with a 30-foot sailboat, a diesel-powered motor home with three slide-outs, and an exotic resort in Tahiti. The result was that their families maintained their enthusiasm and support for the business as they saw the goals realized—one by one!

Your personal Vision Board may include your ideal house or car, a picture of the college diploma that is in your child's future, or multiple pictures of insurance stores, depicting the fact that you recognize that a single store can be grown into an enterprise.

Of course, an important component of getting what you want in life has to do with the beliefs, attitudes, and actions that can't be depicted on your Vision Board. How do you illustrate planning, people management, training, or future change through photographs? You don't. But these matters are all essential to your vision. And with your vision clearly in front of you, you will diminish your chances of "missing it by that much!"

An eagerness to learn, and then apply what you learn, is also essential to achieving your dream. There are two fundamental ways in which we learn:

- Trial and error
- Mimicking success

If you believe that trial and error is the ideal way for you to learn, you should probably stop reading right now, turn on your TV, and watch some so-called "reality" show. You don't have enough time to learn everything you need to know by trial and error, so just resign yourself to "missing it by that much."

Mimicking success is a much more productive way to learn. Someone else has already gone through the trial and error stage for you, so all you have to do is mimic the things he or she has done to become a success.

In your case, it means studying the operations and techniques of successful insurance store-owners and following their blueprint.

If you decide to become a Fiesta Auto Insurance franchisee, I can guarantee you that you have a solid model to mimic. Trust me when I say that I've personally made enough mistakes through trial and error to fill two lifetimes. Fiesta University is our solution to training our owners to become—and remain—successful. It's one key to helping our owners follow best practices and avoid missteps. We have tried to share our training solutions in this book, so that you, as an independent insurance store owner, can achieve the same measure of success.

Remember, too, that we can all continue to learn, no matter how proficient we become. Tiger Woods, arguably the best golfer in the world, still uses a "swing coach." Prior to Phil Jackson's retirement,

Kobe Bryant, a bona fide basketball star, never failed to listen to and take his coach's advice.

Finally, to achieve your dreams, surround yourself—if possible—with people who have achieved *their* dreams. Envision yourself as becoming at least as successful as the successful people you come to know! ❧

On the Subject of Money

Michael E. Gerber

There are three faithful friends: an old wife, an old dog, and ready money.
—Benjamin Franklin

Had Marcos and Teresa first considered the subject of money as we will here, their lives could have been radically different.

Money is on the tip of every entrepreneur's tongue, on the edge (or at the very center) of every entrepreneur's thoughts, intruding on every part of an entrepreneur's life. This is especially true in the case of the insurance store owner, whose cash flow is dependent on new customers walking in the door.

With money consuming so much energy, why do so few entrepreneurs handle it well? What is it about money that is so elusive, so complicated, and so difficult to control? Why is it that every new entrepreneur I've ever met hates to deal with the subject of money? Why are they almost always too late in facing money problems? And why are they constantly obsessed with the desire for more of it?

Money—you can't live with it and you can't live without it. But you better understand it and get your team to understand it. Because until you do, money problems will gnaw at your business...and destroy what peace of mind you possess.

You don't need an accountant or financial planner to do the work I'm proposing. You simply need to prod your people to relate to money very personally. Everyone in your insurance store should understand the financial impact of what they do every day in relationship to the profit and loss of the business.

And so you must teach your people to think like owners, not like agents or administrators. You must teach them to operate like personal profit centers, with a sense of how their work fits in with the business as a whole.

You must involve everyone in the business with the topic of money—how it works, where it goes, how much is left, and how much everybody gets at the end of the day. You also must teach them about the four kinds of money created by the enterprise.

The Four Kinds of Money

In the context of owning, operating, developing, and exiting from an insurance store business, money can be split into four distinct but highly integrated categories:

- Income
- Profit
- Flow
- Equity

Failure to distinguish how the four kinds of money play out in your business is a surefire recipe for disaster.

Important note: Do not talk to your accountants or bookkeepers about what follows; it will only confuse them and you. The information comes from the real-life experiences of thousands of small business owners, most of whom were hopelessly confused about money when I met them. Once they understood and accepted the following principles, they developed clarity about money that could only be called enlightened. Your accountants and bookkeepers may be just as confused about money issues as your co-workers in your store; if this is so, it wouldn't surprise me in the least.

The First Kind of Money: Income

Income is the money that your insurance store takes in by selling and renewing policies every day. Obviously, this is in the form of commissions from the companies for whom you write the policies. But income has nothing to do with *ownership*. Income is solely the province of *employee-ship*. It doesn't matter what you own if your team isn't writing policies.

The Second Kind of Money: Profit

Profit is what's left over after your team has done its job effectively and efficiently—selling insurance policies to a sufficient number of prospects to take in more money than it costs to operate your insurance store. If there is no profit, the business is doing something wrong.

However, just because the business shows a profit does not mean it is necessarily doing all the right things in the right way. Instead, it just means that something was done right during or preceding the period in which the profit was earned.

The important issue here is whether the profit was intentional or accidental. If it happened by accident (which is the case with most profit in most small businesses), don't take credit for it. You'll live to regret your impertinence.

If the profit occurred intentionally, take all the credit you want. You've earned it. Because profit created intentionally, rather than by accident, is replicable—again and again. And your business's ability to repeat its performance is the most critical ability it can have.

As you'll soon see, the value of money is a function of your store's ability to produce it in predictable amounts at an above-average return on investment. Profit can be understood only in the context of your business's purpose, as opposed to *your* purpose as an owner. Profit, then, fuels the forward motion of the business that produces it. This is accomplished in four ways:

- Profit is *investment capital* that feeds and supports growth.
- Profit is *bonus capital* that rewards people for exceptional work.
- Profit is *operating capital* that shores up money shortfalls.
- Profit is *return-on-investment* capital that rewards you, the insurance store owner, for taking risks.

Without profit, your business cannot subsist, much less grow. Profit is the fuel of progress.

If a business misuses or abuses Profit, however, the penalty is much like having no profit at all. Imagine the plight of an entrepreneur who has way too much return-on- investment capital and not enough investment capital, bonus capital, and operating capital. Can you see the imbalance this creates?

The Third Kind of Money: Flow

Flow is what money *does* in a business, as opposed to what money *is*. Whether the business is large or small, money tends to move erratically through it, much like a pinball. One minute it's there; the next minute it's not.

Flow can be even more critical to survival than profit, because a business can produce a profit and still be short of money. Has this ever happened to you? It's called *profit on paper*, rather than in fact.

No matter how large your business, if the money isn't there when it's needed, you're threatened—regardless of how much profit you've made. You can borrow it, of course. But money acquired in dire circumstances is almost always the most expensive kind of money you can get.

Knowing where the money is and where it will be when you need it is a critically important task.

Generally, two issues, and two issues alone, doom small businesses: short-term cash flow problems and long-term cash flow problems. Otherwise you have little to worry about.

Rules of Flow

You will learn no more important lesson than the huge impact flow can have on the health and survival of your business or enterprise. The following two rules will help you understand why this subject is so critical.

1. **The First Rule of Flow states that your Income Statement is static, while the Flow is dynamic.** Your income statement is a snapshot, while the flow is a moving picture. So, while your income statement is an excellent tool for analyzing your business after the fact, it's a poor tool for managing it in the heat of the moment.

Your income statement tells you (1) how much money you're spending and where, and (2) how much money you're receiving and from where.

Flow gives you the same information as the income statement, plus it tells you when you're spending and receiving money. In other words, flow is an income statement moving through time. And that is the key to understanding flow. It is about management in real time. How much is coming in? How much is going out? You'd like to know this daily, or even by the hour, if possible. Never by the week or month.

You must be able to forecast flow. You must have a flow plan that helps you gain a clear vision of the money that's out there next month and the month after that. You must also pinpoint what your needs will be in the future.

Ultimately, however, when it comes to flow, the action is always in the moment. It's about now!

Unfortunately, few entrepreneurs pay any attention to flow until it dries up completely and slow pay becomes no pay. They are oblivious to this kind of detail until, say, the walk-in traffic to the store dries up because of changes in the economy. That gets an entrepreneur's attention because the expenses keep on coming.

When it comes to flow, most business people are flying by the proverbial seat of their pants. No matter how many people you hire to take care of your money, until you change the way you think about it, you will always be out of luck. No one can do this for you.

Managing flow takes attention to detail. But when flow is managed, your life takes on an incredible sheen. You're in charge! You're swimming with the current, not against it.

2. **The Second Rule of Flow states that money seldom moves as you expect it to.** But you do have the power to change that, provided you understand the two primary sources of money as it comes in and goes out of your insurance store.

The truth is, the more control you have over the *source* of money, the more control you have over its flow. The sources of money are both inside and outside of your business.

Money comes from outside your business in the form of receivables, investments, and loans.

Money comes from *inside* your business in the form of payables, taxes, capital investments, and payroll. These are the costs associated with attracting business, delivering your services, operations, and so forth.

Few insurance store owners see the money going *out* of their business as a source of money, but it is.

When considering how to spend money in your business, you can save—and therefore make—money in three ways:

- Do it more effectively.
- Do it more efficiently.
- Stop doing it altogether.

By identifying the money sources inside and outside of your business, and then applying these methods, you will be immeasurably better at controlling the flow in your business. But what are these sources? They include how you

- manage your services;
- compensate your people;
- plan people's use of time;
- determine the direct cost of your services;
- decrease the time you spend seeing individual clients through more efficient presentations;
- manage your work;
- collect account receivables; and
- countless more.

In fact, every task performed in your business (and ones you haven't yet learned how to perform) can be done more efficiently and effectively, dramatically reducing the cost of doing business. In the process, you will create more income, produce more profit, and balance the flow.

The Fourth Kind of Money: Equity

Sadly, few entrepreneurs fully appreciate the value of equity in their businesses. Yet, equity is the second most valuable asset any insurance store entrepreneur will ever possess. (The first most valuable asset is, of course, your life. More on that later.)

Equity is the financial value placed on your insurance store by a prospective buyer of your store.

Thus, your *store* is your most important product, not your services. Because your store has the power to set you free. That's right. Once you sell your business—providing you get what you want for it—you're free!

Of course, to enhance your equity, to increase your store's value, you have to build a business that works. A business that can become a true business and a business that can become a true enterprise. A practice/business/enterprise that can produce income, profit, flow, and equity better than any other practice/business/enterprise can.

To accomplish that, your business must be designed so that it can do what it does systematically and predictably, every single time.

The Story of McDonald's

Let me tell you the most unlikely story anyone has ever told you about the successful building of a business and, ultimately, an enterprise. Let me tell you the story of Ray Kroc, the founder of McDonald's.

You might be thinking, "What on earth does a hamburger stand have to do with an insurance store? I'm not in the hamburger business; I'm in the insurance business." Yes, you are. But, after all, McDonald's is basically a store, and by learning from McDonald's, *your* store—and your life—are going to be transformed.

In Ray Kroc's story lies the answer.

Ray Kroc called his first McDonald's restaurant "a little money machine." That's why thousands of franchisees bought it. And the reason it worked? Ray Kroc demanded consistency. So that a hamburger in Philadelphia would be an advertisement for one in Peoria. In fact, no matter where you bought a McDonald's hamburger in the 1950s, the meat patty was guaranteed to weigh exactly 1.6 ounces, with a diameter of 3 ⅝ inches. It was in the McDonald's handbook.

Did Ray Kroc succeed? You know he did! And so can you, once you understand his methods. Consider just one part of Ray Kroc's story.

In 1954, Ray Kroc made his living selling the five-spindle Multimixer milkshake machine. He heard about a hamburger stand in San Bernardino, California, which had eight of his machines in operation, meaning it could make 40 shakes simultaneously. That he had to see.

Kroc flew from Chicago to Los Angeles and then drove 60 miles to San Bernardino. As he sat in his car outside Mac and Dick McDonald's restaurant, he watched as lunch customers lined up for bags of hamburgers.

In a revealing moment, Kroc approached a strawberry blonde in a yellow convertible. As he later described it, "It was not her sex appeal but the obvious relish with which she devoured the hamburger that made my pulse begin to hammer with excitement."

Passion.

In fact, it was the French fry that truly captured his heart. Before the 1950s, it was almost impossible to buy fries of consistent quality. Ray Kroc changed all that. "The French fry," he once wrote, "would become almost sacrosanct for me, its preparation a ritual to be followed religiously."

Passion and preparation.

The potatoes had to be "just so"—top-quality Idaho russets, 8 ounces apiece, deep-fried to a golden brown, and salted with a shaker that, as Kroc put it, kept going "like a Salvation Army girl's tambourine."

As Kroc soon learned, potatoes too high in water content—and even top-quality Idaho russets varied greatly in water content—will come out soggy when fried. And so Kroc sent out teams of workers, armed with hydrometers, to make sure all his suppliers were producing potatoes in the optimal solids range of 20 to 23 percent.

Preparation and passion. Passion and preparation. Look those words up in the dictionary, and you'll see Ray Kroc's picture. Can you envision your picture there?

Do you understand what Ray Kroc did? Do you see why he was able to sell thousands of franchises? Kroc knew the true value of equity, and, unlike Marcos from our story, Kroc went to work *on* his business, rather than *in* his business. He knew the hamburger wasn't his product—McDonald's was!

So what does *your* insurance store need to do to become a little money machine? What is the passion that will drive you to build a business that works—a turnkey system like Ray Kroc's? John has solid ideas—and a solid plan—on how that can and will work for you.

Equity and the Turnkey System

What's a turnkey system? And why is it so valuable to you? To better understand it, let's look at another example of a turnkey system that worked to perfection: the recordings of Frank Sinatra.

Frank Sinatra's records were to him as McDonald's restaurants were to Ray Kroc. They were part of a turnkey system that allowed Sinatra to sing to millions of people without having to be there himself.

Sinatra's recordings were a dependable turnkey system that worked predictably, systematically, automatically, and effortlessly to produce the same results every single time—no matter where they were played, and no matter who was listening.

Regardless of where Frank Sinatra was, his records just kept on producing income, profit, flow, and equity, over and over . . . and they still do! Sinatra needed only to produce the prototype recording and the system did the rest.

Kroc's McDonald's is another prototypical turnkey solution, addressing everything McDonald's needs to do in a basic, systematic way so that anyone properly trained by McDonald's can successfully reproduce the same results. And this is where you'll realize your Equity Opportunity: in the way your store does business; in the way your business systematically does what you intend it to do; and in the development of your turnkey system—a system that works even in the hands of ordinary people (and team members less experienced than you) to produce extraordinary results.

Remember, if you want to build vast equity in your business:

- Go to work *on* your business, building it into an enterprise that works every single time.
- Go to work *on* your business to build a totally integrated turnkey system that delivers exactly what you promised every single time.
- Go to work *on* your business to package it and make it stand out from the insurance stores you see everywhere else.

Here is the most important idea you will ever hear about your business and what it can potentially provide for you:

The value of your equity is directly proportional to how well your business works. And how well your business works is directly proportional to the effectiveness of the systems you have put into place upon which the operation of your business depends.

Whether money takes the form of income, profit, flow, or equity, the amount of it—and how much of it stays with you—invariably boils down to this: money, happiness, life—it all depends on how well your business works. Not on your people, not on you, but on the system.

Your business holds the secret to more money. Are you ready to learn how to find it?

There is an inevitable conflict between you as an employee and you as the owner. It's a battle between the part of you working *in* the business and the part of you working *on* the business. Between the part of you working for income and the part of you working for equity.

Here's how to resolve this conflict:

- Be honest with yourself about whether you're filling *employee* shoes or *owner* shoes.
- As your business's key employee, determine the most effective way to do the job you're doing, *and then document that job.*
- Once you've documented the job, create a strategy for replacing yourself with someone else who will then use your documented system exactly as you do.
- Have your new employees manage the newly delegated system. Improve the system by quantifying its effectiveness over time.
- Repeat this process throughout your business whenever you catch yourself acting as employee rather than owner.
- Learn to distinguish between ownership work and employee-ship work every step of the way.

Master these methods, understand the difference between the four kinds of money, develop an interest in how money works in your business, and then watch it flow in!

Now let's take another step in our strategic thinking process. Let's look at the subject of *planning*. But, first, let's read what John has to say about money. ✤

The Answer to More Money–All Four Kinds!

John K. Rost

Money isn't the most important thing in life, but it's reasonably close to oxygen on the "gotta have it" scale.

—Zig Ziglar

Since I first absorbed Michael's thoughts on the four kinds of money, I have asked myself, "How do I make sure that my Fiesta Auto Insurance franchisees—and every other insurance store owner—understands and applies these principles—and how can I make it easier for them to do so?"

Obviously, you don't have to be a Fiesta franchisee to benefit from these principles. Every independent insurance store can utilize these concepts.

1. **Income:** As Michael stated, "Income is the money that your insurance store takes in by selling and renewing policies every day." As the owner of an insurance store, your goal is to make sure that you sell the right kinds of policies—offered by reputable companies—so that you can

best serve your customers. Then you need to follow that up with a selling system…one that enables you to attract prospects and then turn them into satisfied customers.

The bottom line is, in order to have income, you need something to sell, someone to sell it, a "place" to sell it, and systems in place to measure how your store is performing—to make sure that the income stream is both consistent and adequate.

Consistent, of course, means that income is ongoing and dependable. If there are times in the year when sales and income are lower, there must be other times in the year when they are higher.

Adequate simply means that there is enough money coming in to cover your store's operating overhead—rent, payroll, marketing, phones, computers, and outside services. But a successful E-Myth insurance store demands that you make more than adequate income.

2. **Profit:** You make a profit by bringing in more than "adequate" break-even income. Independent insurance stores sometimes struggle with matters such as high overhead, low productivity, and poor management systems. All of these things eat into profit. Generally, clear-cut systems are the answer.

But the idea isn't simply to make a profit. It's to make as much profit as possible.

The challenge, then, is to receive more than we spend. What I didn't say was to spend less than we receive. On the surface, it sounds the same. However, many insurance store owners typically focus on reducing expenses rather than focusing on bringing in unlimited revenue.

Time and time again, I have witnessed business owners prepare their thought processes in ways that are ultimately unproductive. Many of their decisions will be designed to reduce the amount of capital they apply to grow their businesses, instead of applying capital in productive ways that will result in positive returns.

What I'm suggesting is that in most ventures, the owner can only save so much. The rent for an insurance retail store could range from $500 to $2,500 a month—or more. Naturally, rental cost is largely a function of location. What those locations will deliver in terms of sales can be vastly different.

It could be that the $500-monthly rent store and the $2,500-monthly rent store both have room for multiple desks, computers, and phones. They'll likely both have outdoor signage, a clearly identified entrance door, and some nearby parking spaces.

However, how visible and accessible will the store be to the public? How important is that in terms of generating customers? I have witnessed franchise owners decide against a shopping center location supported by significant traffic and anchored by major tenants, in order to spend $1,500 less in rent in a mostly vacant strip mall far away from the nearest major road. It's likely that all the advertising in the world won't drag customers into that Timbuktu location. Very simply, you must use your capital prudently and effectively to give you the greatest positive return over time.

Choosing a poor location is just one example of the steps the technician will take to virtually ensure failure. Underestimating the true cost of creating the business is another.

At Fiesta Auto Insurance, we obviously had the opportunity to first create the system within our own corporate stores. We can rely on past experience to determine the capital needs of our franchisees. We have the ability to see how the system is used positively and negatively in multiple cities and states.

What I'm saying is that it is vital to have a solid idea of what the needs and demands of your business will really be. It is a serious mistake to assume you will be able to create a franchise or open an independent agency with less money than typically required, and still have the opportunity to succeed. The goal is not simply to survive; it is to thrive.

But there's more to the success formula than "location, location, location." It's also a matter of "people, people, people"—something that Michael and I will both discuss in greater detail in the pages ahead.

But again, many will make the decision to "hire on the cheap" for a customer service representative or licensed agent. This simply does not make sense if your dual objectives are income and profit. How can you make a profit if you hire poorly? Your agents are responsible for sales, so you want the best talent you can find. You want inspired talent, because you need a positive rate of return from everyone on your team.

> **3. Flow:** Michael's observations on the flow of money are of vital importance to the insurance store owner. I have seen owners and their teams do a magnificent job of drawing in new customers and writing new policies, only to discover down the road that cash flow has dried up. Flow has truly become erratic.

One of the underlying reasons for this is the way insurance companies pay their brokers. When a new policy is written, it's generally for a one-year term. So, for the sake of simplicity, let's say that the commission on a certain policy is $120. Some companies will pay the lump sum up front right after the contract is submitted. Others will pay the commission monthly: $120 divided by 12 is $10 a month.

Most owners would prefer to take the upfront payment of $120. But what happens when a policy lapses after six months because the customer stopped paying premiums? All of a sudden, the insurance company wants $60 of the up-front commission returned. This, they deduct from additional commissions they may owe. Suddenly, you, the owner, are faced with a "flow" situation.

To control flow, owners have to exercise some judgment as to the prospective reliability of the client, and which company's policies to offer to which clients. They must also understand and accept the fact that the up-front commission paid to them does not actually belong to them—yet. That means that much of the money must be held in a reserve account, and the new BMW will have to wait. Managing flow requires intelligent discipline, and, as Michael states, it demands that you learn how to forecast as accurately as possible, with the full realization that money seldom moves as you expect it to.

Some owners make it worse by selling a policy that only pays "as earned." This is a huge mistake. Your agency can't survive on $10 a month. Take the cash of the gross commission over the paid-as-earned option, whenever possible. So taking $120 commission up front rather than $10 a month as the customer makes a payment will increase your flow.

Your agents must also be aware of how carriers pay commissions. They need to understand what various carriers pay. Carriers not only pay at different levels, but they pay in different ways at different times. There are carriers that pay 10%, 12%, 15%, or 17% (on new business, for example). Now, is the difference between 10% and 15% just 5%? Of course not. It's actually a 50% difference—50% more money—selling the same service. Commission amounts must be understood by you and your agents. Offer the products that pay appropriately so that you can manage your flow.

For example, if you sell a policy to a customer who makes monthly payments of $60, the total annual premium is $720. If you get paid "as earned," a 10% commission will bring in $6 a month, and a 15% commission will bring in $9 a month. But if you sell a policy offered by a company that pays the entire commission up front, a 10% commission will bring in $72, and a 15% commission will bring in $108.

Of course, if the policy cancels six months later, you will have to refund $54 to the carrier. But there is no interest charge, so you will have been able to use that money for 6 months, free of charge.

4. Equity: I believe that every insurance store owner needs to keep in mind that there are two equally viable reasons to own the business. The first is to provide an ongoing income stream, and the second is to build equity for the future. After all, no one wants to work forever (whether *in* or *on* his or her business). Most people I know want to retire eventually—and they want to do so with enough money to enjoy the things in life for which they have invested so much time, money, and energy.

Whether you are a "mom-and-pop" insurance store owner with one or more stores, or you are a Fiesta franchisee with a single or multiple locations, the principle of equity is the same. You want to build something that someone else will want to buy from you for substantially more than your investment. In the insurance industry, I have seen owners sell their store for two million dollars or more. In fact, that future prospect also inspires our owners to open more than one store. Not only do they replicate daily success and income growth through the implementation of systems that are proven to work, but they can also eagerly anticipate that day when the sale of those stores will fund the retirement plans of their dreams.

Part of the reason that the ownership of multiple stores—and the ever-growing equity—works is loosely based on the McDonald's model that Michael addressed in the previous chapter.

Would you have ever heard of McDonald's—would you have ever taken those begging kids of yours to McDonald's for a Happy Meal—if there were only one "Mac and Dick McDonald's" restaurant, and it was in San Bernardino, California? Probably not…unless you lived in San Bernardino.

The reason you've likely bought so many Happy Meals (if you have children), is because Ray Kroc was able to take a single idea and replicate it around the country and, ultimately, around the world. (The little plastic toys included in the Happy Meal didn't hurt!)

Ray Kroc's global business was built on five essentials:

1. A consistent product;
2. Effective training and systems;
3. Brand identity;
4. Competitive pricing; and,
5. Repeat business.

Let's look at them all in terms of McDonald's as a model, and see how they apply to your insurance store—whether it's the one you own today, or the one that you may open as a result of reading this book.

> **1. A Consistent Product.** As Michael pointed out, a hamburger purchased in Philadelphia would be an

advertisement for one in Peoria. In terms of size, weight, and shape, all of the burgers sold in any store were identical to the burgers sold in any other store. Arguably, they aren't the best hamburgers in the world, but there are no surprises when you order one. This is often referred to as "managing expectations."

2. **Effective Training.** The training system at every McDonald's is clear, concise, and carefully structured. All team members are cross-trained in every function, so there is never a gap between what is promised to the customer and what is delivered to the customer...or *how* it is delivered.

3. **Brand Identity**. Everything about a McDonald's says McDonald's, from signage to uniforms to menu boards to packaging. And, of course, all of their advertising supports the brand beautifully.

4. **Competitive Pricing.** Hamburger eaters are not likely to pay three times more for a Big Mac® than they would for a Burger King Whopper®, so McDonald's has to remain competitive with other quick-serve hamburger chains.

5. **Repeat Business.** Can you imagine McDonald's being a multi-billion dollar business if every customer only bought one hamburger and never came back for more? Customer retention and repeat business are essential to every successful business.

All five of the business essentials in play at every McDonald's also apply to the operation of any successful insurance store.

Specifically, at Fiesta, we offer a **consistent product**; we sell auto and homeowners policies from the best companies in the business, and we provide optional tax preparation services for our clients. The beauty of tax preparation services is that the client comes in, turns over his or her records, answers some questions, and we can do the actual calculations and complete the forms at a time when there is less traffic at the store—or even after hours. The exact same products and services are offered by every store, unless, for some reason, certain insurance companies do not operate in certain states or cities.

We have an established system of **effective training** that ensures the success of every Fiesta Auto Insurance store. This training is not an afterthought: I put it in place when I only had one store, and now it's available online through Fiesta University. As an independent, your training must be exact, detailed, and consistent. You may not need a "university" to accomplish this, but you might need a "trainer," (even if that means you), and a well-written training manual.

Brand identity is also very important. Many independent insurance stores simply have a sign that says "Insurance," and they display posters from the companies they represent—or, worse yet, travel posters that have nothing to with insurance. All the posters in our stores (and we do believe in posters and signage) are branded with the Fiesta name. Your independent store should be branded with *your* name, not those of insurance carriers. Your sign should have your name, not just the word "Insurance." That would be like McDonald's putting up a sign that simply says "Burgers and Fries." You must be conscious of building your brand.

I'll be telling you more about the Fiesta target market later, but we realize that **competitive pricing** is very important to our market, so we work with our affiliated companies to make sure that happens.

Finally, in the insurance industry, **repeat business** means that we have to manage cancellations and reinstate lapsed policies, plus, we have to seek and earn referral business.

All of these things are not just plans or hopes. They are established systems, upon which we have built our success.

But there's one more component that could be essential to your success... and it's a BIG one that I've already mentioned. It is beneficial to you that you own more than one store.

One person could own more than one McDonald's, and he or she would not have to be at every location every day. I recently met a McDonald's franchisee who has twelve McDonald's franchises. And I guarantee you that she works *on* her business, not *in* her business. She does not stop in at each of her McDonald's every day. Another individual I met owns more than 400 Subway franchises. Can you imagine visiting 400 Subways on any given day? Yet all stores function beautifully because solid systems are in place.

The same principle applies in the operation of an insurance store with the same positive outcome that owning multiple McDonald's or Subway stores provides.

Our goal is to help our owners/franchisees maximize income and profit, manage flow, and build equity by offering a turnkey system that is virtually fail-safe.

Money, happiness, life—they all depend on how well your business works for you. Not on your people, not on you, but on the system—on the E-Myth Way! ✤

On the Subject of Planning

Michael E. Gerber

Luck is good planning, carefully executed.

—Anonymous

Another obvious oversight revealed in Marcos and Teresa's story was the absence of true planning.

Every person starting his or her own business must have a plan. Someone lacking a vision is simply someone who goes to work every day. Someone who is just doing it, doing it, doing it. Busy, busy, busy. Maybe making money, maybe not. Maybe getting something out of life, maybe not. Taking chances without really taking control.

The plan tells anyone who needs to know *how we do things here.* The plan defines the objective and the process by which you will attain it. The plan encourages you to organize tasks into functions, and then helps people grasp the logic of each of those functions. This in turn permits you to bring new employees up to speed quickly.

There are numerous books and seminars on the subject of business management, but I want to teach you something else that you've never been taught before: how to be a manager and an entrepreneur. It has nothing to do with conventional insurance store management and everything to do with thinking like an entrepreneur.

The Planning Triangle

The trouble with most small companies is that they are dependent on the owner. They are formed around the technician, whether an attorney, or roofer, or chiropractor, or insurance agent.

You may choose in the beginning to start an insurance store, but you should understand its limitations. The company called an *insurance store* depends on the owner—that is, you. The company called a *business* depends on other people plus a system by which that business does what it does. Once your store becomes a business, you can replicate it, turning it into an *enterprise*.

Is your company going to be an office, a business, or an enterprise? Planning is crucial to answering this all-important question. Whatever you choose to do must be communicated by your plan, which is really three interrelated plans in one. We call it the Planning Triangle, and it consists of:

- the Business plan;
- the Job plan; and
- the Completion plan.

The three plans form a triangle, with the business plan at the base, the job plan in the center, and the completion plan at the apex.

The business plan determines *who* you are (the business), the job plan determines *what* you do (the specific focus of your real estate business), and the completion plan determines *how* you do it (the fulfillment process).

The
Completion
Plan

The Store Plan

The Business Plan

By looking at the Planning Triangle, we see that the three critical plans are interconnected. The connection between them is established by asking the following questions:

1. *Who are we?*—purely a strategic question
2. *What do we do?*—both a strategic and a tactical question
3. *How do we do it?*—both a strategic and a tactical question

Strategic questions shape your business's vision and destiny, of which your business is only one essential component. Tactical questions turn that vision into reality. Thus, strategic questions provide the foundation for tactical questions, just as the base provides the foundation for the middle and apex of your Planning Triangle.

First ask: What do we do and how do we do it *strategically?* And then: What do we do and how do we do it *practically?*

Let's look at how the three plans will help you develop your business.

The Business Plan

Your business plan will determine what you choose to do in your insurance store and the way you choose to do it. Without a business plan, your operation can do little more than survive. And even that will take more than a little luck.

Without a business plan you're treading water in a deep lake with no shore in sight. You're working against the natural flow.

I'm not talking about the traditional business plan that is taught in business schools. No, this business plan reads like a story—the most important story you will ever tell.

Your business plan must clearly describe:

- the business you are creating;
- the purpose it will serve;
- the vision it will pursue;
- the process through which you will turn that vision into a reality; and
- the way money will be used to realize your vision.

Build your business plan with *business* language, not *insurance* language. Make sure the plan focuses on matters of interest to your lenders and shareholders rather than just your technicians. It should rely on demographics and psychographics to tell you who buys and why; it should also include projections for return on investment and return on equity. Use it to detail both the market and the strategy through which you intend to become a leader in that market, not as an insurance store but as a business enterprise.

The business plan, though absolutely essential, is only one of three critical plans every entrepreneur needs to create and implement. Now let's take a look at the store plan.

The Store Plan

The store plan includes everything a broker needs to know, have, and do to deliver his or her promise to a client or agent on time, every time. Every task should prompt you to ask three questions:

1. What do I need to know?
2. What do I need to have?
3. What do I need to do?

What Do I Need to Know?

What information do I need to satisfy my promise on time, every time, exactly as promised? In order to recognize what you need to know, you must understand the expectations and limitations of others. Are you clear on those expectations? Don't make the mistake of assuming you know. Instead, create a need-to-know checklist to make sure you ask all the necessary questions.

A need-to-know checklist might look like this:

- What are the expectations of my insurance company providers? (The companies whose policies I sell.)
- What are the expectations of my team members?
- What are the expectations of my customers?
- What are the expectations of my outside support providers?

What Do I Need to *Have?*

This question raises the issue of resources—namely, money, people, and time. If you don't have enough money to finance operations, how can you fulfill those expectations without creating cash-flow problems? If you don't have a sufficient number of people or people with sufficient skills, what happens then?

And if you don't have enough time to manage the job to completion, what happens when you can't be in two places at once?

Don't assume that you can get what you need when you need it.
Most often, you can't. And even if you can get what you need at the
last minute, you will pay dearly for it.

What Do I Need to Do?

The focus here is on actions to be started and finished. What do
I need to do to fulfill the expectations of my clients on time, every
time, exactly as promised? Answering the question *What do I need
to do?* requires a series of action plans, including:

- the objective to be achieved;

- the standards by which you will know that the objective
  has been achieved;

- the benchmarks you need to reach in order for the
  objective to be achieved;

- the function/person accountable for the completion of
  the benchmarks;

- the budget for the completion of each benchmark; and

- the time by which each benchmark must be completed.

Your action plans should become the foundation for the
completion plans. And the reason you need completion plans is
to assure that everything you do is not only realistic, but can also
be managed.

The Completion Plan

If the store plan gives you results and provides you with standards, the completion plan tells you everything you need to know

about every benchmark in the store plan—that is, how you're going to fulfill client expectations on time, every time, as promised.

The completion plan is essentially the operations manual, providing information about the details of doing tactical work. It is a guide to tell the people responsible for doing that work exactly how to do it.

Every completion plan becomes a part of the knowledge base of your business. No completion plan goes to waste. Every completion plan becomes a kind of textbook that explains to new employees joining your team how your store operates in a way that distinguishes it from all other insurance businesses.

To return to an earlier example, the completion plan for making a Big Mac is explicitly described in the *McDonald's Operation Manual*, as is every completion plan needed to run a McDonald's business.

The completion plan for your store might include the best tactics for closing a sale, specific follow-up procedures, or the most effective ways to reinstate lapsed policies. Your plan will likely be different—and have to be better—than the plans in place in your competitor's stores. You must constantly raise the questions: *How do we do it here? How should we do it here?*

The quality of your answers will determine how effectively you distinguish your business from every other competitor.

Benchmarks

You can measure the movement of your business—from what it is today to what it will be in the future—using business benchmarks. These are the goals you want your business to achieve during its lifetime.

Your benchmarks should include the following:

- Financial benchmarks
- Emotional benchmarks (the impact your business will have on everyone who comes into contact with it)
- Performance benchmarks

- Client benchmarks (Who are they? Why do they come to you? What will your insurance business give them that no one else does?)
- Employee benchmarks (How do you grow people? How do you find people who want to grow? How do you create a school in your insurance business that will teach your people skills they can't learn anywhere else?)

Your business benchmarks will reflect: (1) the position your store will hold in the minds and hearts of your provider companies, clients, and employees; and (2) how you intend to make that position a reality through the systems you develop.

Your benchmarks will describe how your team will take shape and what systems you will need to develop so that your employees, just like McDonald's employees, will be able to produce the results for which they will be held accountable.

Benefits of the Planning Triangle

By implementing the Planning Triangle, you will discover:
- what your business will look, act, and feel like when it's fully evolved;
- when that's going to happen;
- how much money you will make; and
- much, much more.

These, then, are the primary purposes of the three critical plans: (1) to clarify precisely what needs to be done to get what you want from your business and life; and (2) to define the specific steps by which it will happen.

First *this* must happen, then *that* must happen. One, two, three. By monitoring your progress, step by step, you can determine whether you're on the right track.

That's what planning is all about. It's about creating a standard—a yardstick—against which you will be able to measure your performance.

Failing to create such a standard is like throwing a straw into a hurricane. Who knows where that straw will land?

Have you taken the leap? Have you accepted that the word *business* and the word *store* are not synonymous? That a store relies on you and a business relies on other people plus a system?

Now let's take the next step in our strategic odyssey and take a closer look at the subject of *management*. But, before we do, let's listen to what John has to say on the subject of planning. ✤

What Is a Business Plan?

John K. Rost

Planning is an unnatural process; it is much more fun to do something.
The nicest thing about not planning is that failure comes as a complete
surprise, rather than being preceded by a period of worry and depression.
—Sir John Harvey-Jones

As Michael has clearly illustrated, it takes planning to move your new or existing venture toward success. The three-tier plan he outlined in the Planning Triangle—The Business Plan, The Store Plan, and The Completion Plan—is essential. Yet some people start their ventures without a business plan. My question would be, "How will you know *when* or *if* you become successful?"

Others start their businesses with highly detailed, largely inflexible plans. My question to them is, "What do you do if and when you get broadsided by the unexpected—as you most certainly will be?"

The solution to both of these issues is simply this: build your business on the principles of the Planning Triangle. In each of the three areas, you can allow room for change.

I tend to think of a business plan more in terms of the lava flowing from a volcano, rather than the mountain from which the lava flows. The lava changes form and shape, but the observer knows the basic direction in which it will flow, and knows it will eventually turn from its molten, flowing state into solid rock. But the mountain basically retains the same shape, even after "blowing its top off."

To me, a business plan is both a road map and a GPS. A meaningful plan shows you the possible routes and highlights the milestones on your journey, just as a map does. A meaningful plan also shows you where you are at any given point in time, just as a GPS does. By using both a map and a GPS, you won't have to ask the questions "Where are we going?" and "Are we there yet?" You will know the answers to those questions at all times.

Broken down into its simplest, most basic components, a good business plan asks and answers these essential questions:

- Why am I starting (or did I start) this business?
- What is my starting point? Where am I right now, at the beginning of this journey?
- Where do I want to go with my business? What are my objectives, my goals, and my overall direction?
- What do I need to do to get there? What do I need in terms of people, an outside support team, facilities, equipment, marketing tools, and ongoing income/profit/cash flow to reach my goals?
- What will I do after I get there—after I achieve my initial objectives? Will I open additional stores? Will I sell my store(s) and realize the benefits of the equity I built?

Your business plan is not only useful in terms of guiding your actions (and, hopefully, even avoiding your impulses); it is also useful in sharing your vision with your team. It takes an inspired team to produce the desired results.

If you decide to become a new franchisee with Fiesta Auto Insurance, the issue of a business plan is simple. Most of it has already been created and defined so that you can simply move forward. The important thing for a franchise owner to remember—no matter what the franchise—is that you bought into an existing and already tried and proven business plan. Attempting to turn a McDonald's into a pizza delivery store will not work. If you become affiliated with Fiesta Auto Insurance, we will encourage you to adhere to our proven model for success and FTS—"Follow the System."

Our system is both the owner's road map and GPS. By following the system, the questions of "Where am I?" and "Are we there yet?" should never go unanswered. You will likely always know, because others have gone before you and, in effect, blazed the trail for you… much like the early explorers who blazed new trails all across North America…or Sir Edmund Hillary, who first conquered the steep slopes of Mt. Everest— and whom I followed much later. But it was his proven trail that I followed.

For those of you who choose to operate on your own as a "mom-and-pop," I offer the following basics of planning. You will, of course, want to wrap your entire business plan, store plan, and completion plan around these basics.

The first thing you need to define is your name. What will you call your agency and why? The why is an important question to answer. I've seen countless independent stores hang a sign above their door that simply says "Insurance." I can't imagine how that would induce anyone to walk into the store. There is nothing about the word "Insurance" that sets you apart from other stores and storefronts that display the word "Insurance." There is no "why."

There are very clear, carefully considered reasons why we named our company "Fiesta Auto Insurance," why we chose a specific color palette, why we encourage our franchisees to choose highly targeted locations for their stores, and why we insist that they do not attempt to deviate from our market-tested, fully proven plan. It has to do with our target market and the way our customers view the world—but I'll delve into the "why" of that topic in more detail later on.

The point is, you must develop an identity to stand out from the dismal, unimaginative crowd. And you must know enough about the demographics and your target customers to ask and answer the "why."

The second thing to define is your physical location. Demographics, traffic counts, and the types of businesses that surround you are all important. You can't survive without viable customers, and if you are going to rely on "walk-in" customers, you can't draw those customers into your store without a viable location.

The third thing to consider is what I call your "pro forma." To me, this is a question, followed by specific answers.

Here's the basic pro forma for an insurance store: "How much insurance must I sell, at what specific cost, at what commission rate, with what retention rate, to how many customers, over what period of time, in order to stay in business? And how far beyond that do I need to go to make a profit?" The "how much" is generally stated in types and numbers of policies. The "specific cost" is generally dictated by the provider insurance companies you represent. However, you should know the average premiums that will be collected. "Margins" (or gross profits) are generally the function of your operating overhead. Higher rent or higher employee costs (or any of a number of other things) will reduce your margin. So part of your business plan must be your budget, and it must be controlled (but not over-controlled to the point where you are "a penny wise and a pound foolish"). More on that later.

The component of the pro forma over which you are likely to have the most control is "to how many customers."

This is a function of several things: hours of operation and the convenience of those hours for your potential customers, availability of agents at the right times to meet customers' needs, and your ability to draw prospects into your store. Among the "tools" to consider are:

- Attractiveness of the storefront and the interior;
- Store name, main sign, and additional signage;
- Location of the store in terms of main freeway or arterial access;

- Marketing ploys and tactics; and
- Above all, the ability of your agents to close sales, and then sustain long-term relationships with customers. I see this as a function of both training and hiring selection/natural ability. Both should be considerations in your business practices. Personable, outgoing, well-groomed, so-called "born salespeople" are out there if you look for them.

The last component of your pro forma is "over what period of time." Some businesses—though not very many!—look at the targets and the numbers on an annual or quarterly basis. Many look at them on a monthly or weekly basis. But if you plan to be successful, you need to look at them on a daily basis. "Over what period of time" means TODAY. This is the fastest, most direct way to spot trends and fix problems. And it's not all that big of a challenge if you have the right system in place.

If you achieve the bare minimum requirements of the pro forma, you will break even and probably stay in business. If you don't meet them, you will fail. If you exceed them, you will make a profit and you will want to own more stores. It's as simple as that. It all comes down to the systems you have in place.

Systems are an essential part of an effective business plan. I believe in them completely. They are, for me, the E-Myth Way! ✤

On the Subject
of Management

Michael E. Gerber

*"Management" means, in the last analysis, the substitution of thought
for brawn and muscle, of knowledge for folklore and superstition, and
of cooperation for force*
　　　　　　　　　　　　—Peter Drucker, *People and Performance*

E very owner, including Marcos, eventually faces management
issues. Yet most face them badly.

　　　Why do so many entrepreneurs suffer from a kind of
paralysis when it comes to dealing with the topic of management?
Why are so few able to get their businesses to work the way they want
it to and to run it on time?

The main problem is that, more often than not, the owner doesn't
think like a manager because he doesn't think he *is* a manager. He's an
owner! He rules the roost. He may even hire an office manager to take care
of stuff like scheduling, keeping his calendar, collecting receivables, hiring/
firing, and much more. But he is the king, and the king can do no wrong.

No matter who does the managing, owners usually have a completely inaccurate idea of what it means to manage. They're trying to manage people in a way that is contrary to what is needed. (To the extent that they're even focused on the concept at all.)

We often hear that a good manager must be a "people person." Someone who loves to nourish, figure out, support, care for, teach, baby, monitor, mentor, direct, track, motivate, and—if all else fails— threaten or beat up his or her employees.

Don't believe it. Management has far less to do with people than you've been led to believe.

In fact, despite the claims of every management book written by management gurus (who have seldom managed anything), no one— with the exception of a few bloodthirsty tyrants—has ever learned how to manage people. And the reason is simple: *People are almost impossible to manage.*

Yes, it's true. People are unmanageable. They're inconsistent, unpredictable, unchangeable, unrepentant, irrepressible, and generally impossible.

Doesn't knowing this make you feel better? Now you understand why you've had all those problems! Do you feel the relief, the heavy stone lifted from your chest?

The time has come to fully understand what management is really all about. Rather than managing *people*, management is really all about managing a *process*, a step-by-step way of doing things, which, combined with other processes, becomes a system. For example:

- The process for scheduling;
- The process for answering the telephone;
- The process for greeting a client;
- The process for quoting and selling a client.

Thus, a process is the step-by-step way of doing something over time. Considered as a whole, these processes are a system:

- The on-time scheduling system;
- The telephone answering system;

- The client selling system; and
- The file organization system.

Instead of managing people, then, the truly effective manager has been taught a system for managing a process through which people get things done.

More precisely, managers and their people, *together*, manage the processes—the systems—that comprise your business. Management is less about *who* get things done in your business than about *how* things get done.

In fact, great managers are not fascinated with people but with how things get done through people. Great managers are masters at figuring out how to get things done effectively and efficiently by people using extraordinary systems. You don't need to be Vince Lombardi, his heart on his sleeve as he coached the Green Bay Packers.

Instead, you need to be Tom Landry, displaying the cool and resolve from his background as a bomber pilot during World War II and his engineering degree.

You don't need to wear the fedora on the sidelines. You do need to be clear about your systems, so that your team can do it your way consistently…and win. Great managers constantly ask key questions:

- What is the result we intend to produce?
- Are we producing that result every single time?
- If we're not producing that result every single time, why not?
- If we are producing that result every single time, how could we produce even better results?
- Do we lack a system? If so, what would that system look like if we were to create it?
- If we have a system, why aren't we using it?

And so forth.

In short, a great manager can leave the office fully assured that it will run at least as well as it does when he or she is physically in the room.

Great managers are those who use a great management system. A system that shouts, "This is *how* we manage here!" Not, "This is *who* manages here!"

In a truly effective company, how you manage is always more important than who manages. Provided a system is in place, how you manage is transferable, whereas who manages isn't. How you manage can be taught, whereas who manages can't be.

When a company is dependent on who manages—Murray, Mary, or Moe—that business is in serious jeopardy. Because when Murray, Mary, or Moe leaves, that business has to start over again. What an enormous waste of time and resources!

Even worse, when a company is dependent on who manages, you can bet all the managers in that business are doing their own thing. What could be more unproductive than ten managers who each manage in a unique way? How in the world could you possibly manage those managers?

The answer is: you can't. Because it takes you right back to trying to manage people again. And, as I hope you now know, that's impossible.

In this chapter, I often refer to managers in the plural. I know that most insurance stores only have one manager, the office manager, if they have any at all. And so you may be thinking that a management system isn't so important in a small insurance business. After all, the office manager does whatever an office manager does (and thank God, because you don't want to do it).

But if your store is ever going to turn into the business it could become, and if that business is ever going to turn into the enterprise of your dreams, then the questions you ask about how the office manager manages your affairs are critical ones. Until you come to grips with your dual role as owner and key employee, and the relationship your manager has to those two roles, your practice/business/enterprise will never realize its potential. Thus the need for a management system.

Management System

What, then, is a management system?

The E-Myth says that a management system is the method by which every manager innovates, quantifies, orchestrates, and then monitors the systems through which your business produces the results you expect.

According to the E-Myth, a manager's job is simple:

A manager's job is to invent the systems through which the owner's vision is consistently and faithfully manifested at the operating level of the business.

Which brings us right back to the purpose of your business and the need for an entrepreneurial vision.

Are you beginning to see what I'm trying to share with you? That your business is one single thing? And that all the subjects we're discussing here—money, planning, management, and so on—are all about doing one thing well? That one thing is what your insurance store is intended to do: distinguish your insurance business from all others.

It is the manager's role to make certain it all fits. And it's your role as entrepreneur to make sure your manager knows what the business is supposed to look, act, and feel like when it's finally done. As clearly as you know how, you must convey to your manager what you know to be true—your vision; your picture of the business when it's finally done. In this way, your vision is translated into your manager's marching orders every day he or she reports to work.

Unless your manager embraces that vision, you and your people will suffer from the tyranny of routine. And your business will suffer from it, too.

Now let's move on to *people*. As we know, it's people who are causing all our problems. But first, let's listen to what John has to say about management. ✤

What Do I – Can I – Really Manage?

John K. Rost

So much of what we call management consists of making it difficult for people to work.

—Peter Drucker

The typical owner-operated insurance store doesn't have an office manager. That role usually falls to the owner. The problem is, unless that individual has invested a lot of time designing and implementing effective systems (or has adopted established systems), the management of the company will be haphazard at best.

That's why I followed Michael's advice from the very moment I opened my first store, and that's why, as Michael advises, at Fiesta we have developed processes for scheduling; for answering the telephone; for greeting a client; for quoting, selling, and closing; and for organizing client files. They are a part of our established procedures, part of our training manuals, and part of our expectations.

If, as Michael says, "people are almost impossible to manage," then managing a process—a step-by-step way of doing things—and combining it with other processes to create a system, is of prime importance.

Michael also states that a great management system is one that shouts, "This is *how* we manage here," NOT "this is *who* manages here."

The *how* is critically important in the operation of an insurance store, because I believe there are six key areas where the *how*, rather than the *who*, become the "make or break" difference. Doing it well in each of these six essential areas of success is vital:

- Time (This will be covered in a detailed chapter on Time.)
- Money (Information on this topic is scattered throughout the book. We've already partially covered this topic.)
- Facilities (Again, you will see ideas on this topic throughout the book.)
- Activities (Here's where we'll discuss this topic!)
- Procedures (Again, it's time to cover this subject.)
- Customer Expectations (This topic will be covered in the chapter on Clients.)

As you can see, in this chapter, we've narrowed our primary topics as they relate to management down to *activities* and *procedures*. I'm excited about this subject matter, because "doing it right" brings success to the "mom-and-pop" insurance store, as well as to the franchised store.

As difficult as it can be to manage people, it is easier to manage their activities and procedures. I define "activities" in broad terms: "the essential things that must be done to become and remain a successful insurance store."

I define "procedures" in equally broad terms: "the specific things that must be done to complete the essential activities in a timely and efficient manner." Here's a quick example:

An *activity* is meeting with prospective clients, making a presentation, offering a specific policy or policies, encouraging the clients to sign the contract, obtaining a payment, shaking their hand, and seeing them to the door. That specific activity is obviously called SELLING. All of these steps need to be completed in the selling activity.

A *procedure* is double-checking the contract for accuracy, adding the check to the day's deposits, submitting the contract to the insurance carrier, and retaining and filing necessary documents. This procedure (or set of procedures) could be described as ADMINISTRATION.

To look at it in another way, activity is what you *do* in your job, and procedure is the *way* you do it. Both are important, and both can be managed, but not without systems in place.

An important focus of ours has been to spell out the specifics of our selling system—the controls and procedures necessary to achieve success in sales. We followed up the system we established with carefully designed training and ways to ensure accountability.

If an agent isn't closing contracts, it's usually because the agent skipped some of the steps in the system. He or she may have begun with steps one and two, then skipped to step five, followed by steps eight, thirteen, and fifteen. If we can convince the agent that all the steps are there for a reason, and that they have to be followed in precise order, "closing success" naturally follows.

I probably won't be able to convince you that I'm not spouting another sales message for Fiesta, but I am simply attempting to be very honest with you. If you're a "go-it-alone" insurance store owner, chances are you will have to define and manage both activities and procedures on your own. But if you decide to become a Fiesta franchisee, all those aspects of management—and more—have been developed based on E-Myth principles, making your job easier, and giving you more freedom to enjoy life.

It's been said that "Money does not buy things: it buys freedom." I believe that, and I am living, breathing proof of that principle. Keep that mind of yours wide open while Michael teaches us about people in the next chapter. ❖

On the Subject
of People

Michael E. Gerber

*We are not human beings having a spiritual experience. We are spiritual
beings having a human experience.*

—Teilhard de Chardin

Every entrepreneur I've ever met has complained about people.
About employees: "They come in late, they go home early,
they have the focus of an antique camera!"

About provider insurance companies: "They never get back to
me to answer my urgent questions."

About clients: "They forget to pay their premiums, their policies
get cancelled, and then we have to rewrite those policies."

People, people, people. Every entrepreneur's nemesis. And at the
heart of it all are the people who work for you.

"By the time I tell them how to do it, I could have done it twenty times
myself!" "How come nobody listens to what I say?" "Why is it nobody
ever does what I ask them to do?" Does this sound like your situation?

So what's the problem with people? To answer that, think back to the last time you walked into someone else's place of business. What did you see in the people's faces?

Most of the people you see, I'm sure you will agree, are harried. You can see it in their expressions. They're negative. They're bad-spirited. They're humorless. And with good reason. After all, the clients who trudge in and out of most offices each day have a lot to deal with. Whether it's a medical office, an attorney's office, an accountant's office, or an insurance office, they are dealing with their problems. Most of them are worried, angry, or anxious; they may even be terrified or depressed. Thus, the employees of every business are constantly surrounded by unhappy people.

Is it any wonder these employees are disgruntled? They're answering the same questions all day from people who might prefer not to be there.

Working with people brings great joy—and monumental frustration. And so it is with insurance entrepreneurs and their people. But why? And what can we do about it?

Let's look at the typical entrepreneur—who this person is and isn't.

Most are unprepared to use other people to get results. Not because they can't find people, but because they are fixated on getting the results themselves. In other words, most insurance entrepreneurs are not the businesspeople they need to be, but *technicians suffering from an entrepreneurial seizure.*

Am I talking about you? What were you doing before you became an entrepreneur?

Were you an agent working at another insurance agency? A captive agent on a salary or meager commissions?

Didn't you imagine owning your own business as the way out?

Didn't you think that because you knew how to do the technical work—because you knew so much about your company, or rates, or coverage—that you were automatically prepared to create a new business that does that type of work?

Didn't you assume that by creating your own business you could dump the boss once and for all? How else to get rid of that impossible person, the one driving you crazy, the one who never let you do your own thing, the one who was the main reason you decided to take the leap into a business of your own in the first place?

Didn't you start your own insurance business so that you could become your own boss?

And didn't you imagine that once you became your own boss, you would be free to do whatever you wanted to do—and to take home *all* the money?

Honestly, isn't that what you envision? So you went into business for yourself and immediately dove into work.

Doing it, doing it, doing it. Busy, busy, busy.

Until one day you realized (or maybe not) that you were doing all of the work. You were doing everything you knew how to do, plus a lot more you knew nothing about. Building sweat equity, you thought.

In reality, a technician suffering from an entrepreneurial seizure.

You were just hoping to make a decent living in your own business. Actually, you hoped for considerably more than that. You wanted to beat your big competitors at their own game. And sometimes you did earn a nice dollar. But other times you didn't. You were the one signing the checks all right, but they went to other people.

Does this sound familiar? Is it driving you crazy?

Well, relax, because we're going to show you the right way to do it this time.

Read carefully. Be mindful of the moment. You are about to learn the secret you've been waiting for all of your working life.

The People Law

It's critical to know this about the working life of entrepreneurs who own their own businesses: *Without people, you don't own a business, you own a job.* And it can be the worst job in the world because you're working for a lunatic! (Nothing personal—we simply have to face the truth if we're ever going to change things.)

Let me state what every entrepreneur should know: Without people, you're going to have to do it all yourself. Without human help, you're doomed to try to do too much. This isn't a breakthrough idea, but it's amazing how many entrepreneurs ignore the truth. They end up knocking themselves out, 12 to 16 hours a day. They try to do more, but less actually gets done.

The load can double you over and leave you panting. In addition to the work you're used to doing, you may also have to do the books. And the organizing. And the filing. You'll have to do the planning and the scheduling. In a business of your own, the daily minutiae is never-ceasing—as I'm sure you've found out—and until you discover how to get it done by somebody else, it will continue on and on until you're a burned-out husk. Like painting the Golden Gate Bridge, it's endless. Which puts it beyond the realm of human possibility.

But with others helping you, my friend, things will start to drastically improve. If, that is, you truly understand how to engage people in the work you need them to do. When you learn how to do that, when you learn how to replace yourself with other people—people trained in your system—then your business can really begin to grow. Only then will you begin to experience true freedom yourself.

What typically happens is that entrepreneurs, knowing they need help answering the phone, filing, and so on, go out and find people who can do these things. Once they delegate these duties, however, they rarely spend any time with the little things—the general masses. Deep down they feel it's not important *how* these things get done; it's only important *that* they get done.

They fail to grasp the requirement for a system that makes people their greatest asset rather than their greatest liability. A system so reliable that if Mary dropped dead tomorrow, Judy could do exactly what Mary did. That's where the People Law comes in.

The People Law says that each time you add a new person to your business using an intelligent (turnkey) system that works, you expand your reach. And you can expand your reach almost infinitely! People allow you to be everywhere you want to be simultaneously, without actually having to be there in the flesh.

People are to your insurance store what a record was to Frank Sinatra. As we discussed earlier, a Sinatra record could be (and still is) played in a million places at the same time, regardless of where Frank was. And every record sale produced royalties for Sinatra (or his estate).

With the help of other people, Sinatra created a quality recording that faithfully replicated his unique talents, and then made sure it was marketed, distributed, and the revenue managed.

While Sinatra sang "do-be-do-be-do," all you get to do…is do. And the result, alas, is doo-doo.

Your people can do the same thing for you. All you need to do is to create a "recording"—a system—of your unique talents, your special way of selling insurance, and then replicate it, market it, distribute it, and manage the revenue.

Isn't that what successful businesspeople do? Make a "recording" of their most effective ways of doing business? In this way, they provide a turnkey solution to their clients' problems. A system solution that really works.

Doesn't your business offer the same potential for you that records did for Frank Sinatra (and now for his heirs)? The ability to produce income without having to go to work every day?

Isn't that what your people could be for you? The means by which your system for offering insurance policies to your customers could be faithfully replicated?

But first you've got to have a system. You have to create a unique way of doing business that you can teach to your people, that you can manage faithfully, and that you can replicate consistently, just like McDonald's.

Without such a system, without such a "recording," without a unique way of doing business that really works, all you're left with is people doing their own thing. And that is almost always a recipe for chaos. Rather than guaranteeing consistency, it encourages mistake after mistake after mistake.

And isn't that how the problem started in the first place? People doing whatever *they* perceived they needed to do, regardless of what you wanted? People left to their own devices, with no regard for the costs of their behavior? The costs to you?

In other words, people without a system.

Can you imagine what would have happened to Frank Sinatra if he had followed that example? If every one of his recordings had been done differently? Imagine a million different versions of "My Way." It's unthinkable.

Would you buy a record like that? What if Frank was having a bad day? What if he had a sore throat?

Please hear this: the People Law is unforgiving. Without a systematic way of doing business, people are more often a liability than an asset. Unless you prepare, you'll find out too late which ones are which.

The People Law says that without a specific system for doing business, without a specific system for recruiting, hiring, and training your people to use that system, and without a specific system for managing and improving your systems, your business will always be a crapshoot.

Do you want to roll the dice with your business at stake? Unfortunately, that is what most entrepreneurs are doing.

The People Law also says that you can't effectively delegate your responsibilities unless you have something specific to delegate. And that something specific is a way of doing business that works!

Frank Sinatra is gone, but his voice lives on. And someone is still counting his royalties. That's because Sinatra had a system that worked.

Do you? Do you get to *be* as well as to *do*? Do, be, do, be, do? Or are you just *doing*, all day long?

Now let's move on to the subject of associates. But first, let's listen to what John has to say about people. ❧

Critical Staffing Decisions

John K. Rost

Good management consists in showing average people how to do the work of superior people.

—John D. Rockefeller

If your goal is to own and operate a successful insurance store, there are some basic "People Facts" you need to know, understand, and accept. As suggested in that last statement, it's not enough to *know* the facts. It's not enough to *understand* these facts. You must *accept* them!

- FACT #1: Time is as valuable to most people as money. Accept it.

- FACT #2: Customers don't like to wait. And a collection of old magazines in the lobby isn't likely to help them pass the time with pleasure. Accept it.

- FACT #3: They're not really happy about sitting in your office, because buying insurance is not at the top of their list of things they'd like to be doing. Accept it.

- FACT #4: You need agents staffing your office when customers are most likely to walk in. Accept it.

Here's the reality. You can't do anything about Facts 1-3. They are givens. But Fact #4 is something that is within your power to control.

That's because it is possible to accurately predict the times in the day when most customers will show up at your door. You *can* plan for them, and have sufficient staff on hand to meet their needs. If you get it right, you will solve many of the problems caused by Facts 1-3... and you can even make buying insurance a better experience for your customers! That's if, and only if, you effectively deal with Fact #4.

But, being completely candid here, your store will likely open with just one employee: you. At first it will feel like you just "bought a job." You will have to be open when the customers want you to be open. And that means long hours, six days a week.

I've observed owners who will take breaks off the premises during the hours they are supposed to be open. They will hang that cardboard clock in the window...you know, the one that says, "We will return at:" and then the clock hands are set to point to 1:00, or 2:00, or whatever. Or worse, they'll tape a note to the inside of the window: "Back in 15 minutes." Fifteen minutes from *when*, exactly?

If I ever stumble across a franchisee who pulls this stunt, my wrath quickly boils to the surface. There is no excuse for this. No excuse at all.

Obviously, you don't want to spend your entire life as the sole employee of your insurance store. There will come a time (the sooner the better, I think) when you will want to hire additional staff.

There are three major considerations involved here: WHEN to hire, WHO to hire, and WHERE to find them.

In terms of the "When," we have developed a set of financial guideposts so that our owners know that it's safe and advisable to add staff. In the simplest terms, when an agent is writing an average of 75 policies a month, it's generally an appropriate time to hire another agent. When that number hits 125 new policies between the two agents, it's time to add a third...and so on. Of course, we help our franchisees analyze their numbers so that they aren't hiring prematurely just because they desperately want to.

The "Who" is the second important consideration. Here is where many business owners sabotage their success because they fail to hire the right person for the job. For many, their mistake is in hiring a family member or friend of the family for a position he or she is not qualified to fill. Or it may be hiring an individual based on a cheap wage verses the best person at an adequate wage. Why does an owner hire a low-wage and most likely low-skill employee and then place that person directly in front of their valued customers? The owner naively expects this low-wage, low-skilled employee to be a master at sales and customer service and is soon disappointed.

If you've delved into E-Myth books, you know that Michael advocates hiring the person with the "lowest possible skill level required to accomplish the vital tasks of the position."

In the case of an insurance store, that lowest skill level would be a licensed property casualty agent who, in Fiesta's case, also has a couple other specialized skills. (I'll discuss those later.) But, as one example, the candidate needs to be effective at communicating with the customer. So if that person is a licensed agent but is sloppy, has bad manners, never wants to get up from behind the desk and shake hands with people when they walk in, and instead just simply waves people to come sit down, that individual is not likely to succeed.

Many "mom-and-pop" insurance store owners make the mistake of hiring a customer service representative (CSR) instead of a licensed agent. We strongly recommend hiring only licensed agents. As soon as you hire a CSR, that CSR will begin working with customers. It won't be long before he will begin doing things to help the customer that will cross over into activities that only a licensed agent should be handling. The unfortunate thing is, the person they happened to be talking to could be an investigator for the Department of Insurance, and the owner could face a costly hearing, as well as stiff fines. It's not worth it, and once again, you get what you pay for. If you hire a CSR intending that they just open mail, help the customer make a payment, and do odd jobs—and you can hold them to that—it might work. But when a customer asks a question and your CSR responds, "Oh, I can't help you with that. I don't know anything about it," that doesn't sound good. It sounds like your team is incompetent and poorly trained, which may not be the case at all.

The third major staffing consideration is "Where" to find them.

First, a big "don't." DON'T, under any circumstances, put a "Help Wanted" sign in your window. It indicates to the public that you're not professional. (Have you ever seen a "Help Wanted" sign on a bank?) A help wanted sign will only give you an opportunity to waste time with unqualified people who are simply looking for "any" job.

Now that we've made that clear, here are our guidelines on hiring. Obviously, an owner can't hire someone until he or she has someone to interview. How do you find these people?

The old way was simply to run a classified ad in the local newspaper. The times have dramatically changed, however, with the advent of the Internet age. Newspaper classifieds are no longer hoping to operate effectively on their own. Many large newspapers are also linked with an online vehicle, with Monster.com and CareerBuilder.com being two of those available today. Some of the best values in classified advertising are the result of combining a newspaper ad on Sunday with the online vehicle that they are tied with—as a package deal. In this scenario, you receive a small newspaper ad on Sunday and perhaps a thirty-day listing online. The online version will give the owner more space to discuss the needs of the position and highlight the benefits of the job to the prospect.

Be sure to look at the ads of your competitors and write one that is equal or better. Use a salary range from entry level to a superstar wage.

At Fiesta, we have seen very poor results from the free online classifieds such as Craigslist.org and others. Most job postings on this type of site will require limited skills and, as such, are not the type of staff you are looking for. Take a look at these sites and most likely you will not find a posting for a local bank branch manager. Learn from what you are seeing and go where the skilled labor goes to seek a position. The fact that the listings are free is not a reason to post. You will get what you paid for, most likely an employee with no resume and questionable job behavior. Spend your capital wisely and find the best talent at the appropriate wage—not just a body to fill a desk. Once you have talent to interview, how do you make the best hiring decision?

- Hire the staff member based on his or her true talents matched with the requirements of the position. If you are hiring an agent for a nonstandard personal lines agency, don't hire a preferred agent from a captive background. At most insurance stores, the agents will need to understand the underwriting requirements of multiple carriers and will have to be current on that market rating software. Match talent with the position.

- Do your best to keep friends and family out of the business. Friends will no longer be friends and family will assume they can never be fired. Both of these spell disaster for you, the owner. Be disciplined when hiring, and you will be rewarded with a successful business.

- Do not try to break in an unskilled employee unless you have created a system to train unskilled employees. If you have just opened your first location, attempting to develop a training system is not a good use of your time and resources. Search for the talent that has the skills and watch them succeed. Once you have multiple stores and a team of talented staff, then perhaps a system for new unskilled talent can be created.

As Michael says, "Each time you add a new person to your business using an intelligent (turnkey) system that works, you expand your reach. And you can expand your reach almost infinitely! People allow you to be everywhere you want to be simultaneously, without actually having to be there in the flesh."

Over the long term, you can't do it all yourself. Unless of course, you want no social life, no outside interests, and no vacations. In-place systems will guarantee a better life for you! ❧

11

On the Subject of Associates

Michael E. Gerber

Associate yourself with men of good quality if you esteem your own reputation, for 'tis better to be alone than in bad company.
                                                                    —George Washington

If you're a sole practitioner—that is, you're selling only yourself—then your company called an insurance store will never make the leap to a company called a business. The progression from store to business to enterprise demands that you hire other people to do what you do (or don't do).

If you don't know it yet, you will soon learn that additional staff can pose a huge problem. But until you face this special business problem, your store will never become a business, and your business will certainly never become an enterprise.

Long ago, God said, "Let there be insurance agents. And so they never forget who they are in my creation, let them be damned forever to hire people exactly like themselves." Enter their employees.

Why in the world do we do these things to ourselves? Where will this madness lead? It seems the blind are leading the blind, and the blind are paying the blind to lead them. Talk about an approach doomed to fail at the very outset!

It's time to step out of the darkness. It's time to see the world as it really is. It's time to do things that work.

Solving the Employee Problem

Let's say you're about to hire an employee. Someone who has specific skills. It all starts with choosing the right personnel. After all, these are people to whom you are delegating your responsibility and for whose behavior you are completely liable. Do you really want to leave that choice to chance? Are you that much of a gambler? I doubt it.

If you've never worked with your new hire, how do you really know he or she is skilled? For that matter, what does "skilled" mean? An insurance license? Good people skills? Or something more?

For you to make an intelligent decision about this new hire, you must have a working definition of the word *skilled*. Your challenge is to know *exactly* what your expectations are, then to make sure your other people operate with precisely the same expectations. Failure here almost assures a breakdown in your relationship.

I want you to write the following on a piece of paper: "By *skilled*, I mean…." Once you create your personal definition, it will become a standard for you and your business, for your clients, and for your team.

A standard, according to *Webster's Eleventh*, is something "set up and established by authority as a rule for the measure of quantity, weight, extent, value, or quality."

Thus, your goal is to establish a measure of quality control and a standard of skill that you will apply to all your people. More important, you are also setting a standard for the performance of your company.

By creating standards for your selection of others to join your team—standards of skill, performance, integrity, financial stability, and experience—you have begun the powerful process of building an insurance business that can operate exactly as you expect it to.

By carefully thinking about exactly what to expect, you have already begun to improve your business. In this enlightened state, you will see the selection of your team as an opportunity to define what you (1) intend to provide for your clients, (2) expect from your employees, and (3) demand for your life.

Powerful stuff, isn't it? Are you up to it? Are you ready to feel your rising power?

Don't rest on your laurels just yet. Defining those standards is only the first step you need to take. The second step is to create an Employee Development System.

An Employee Development System is an action plan designed to tell you what you are looking for in a team member. It includes the exact benchmarks, accountabilities, timing of fulfillment, and budget you will assign to the process of looking for ideal employees, identifying them, recruiting them, interviewing them, training them, managing their work, auditing their performance, compensating them, reviewing them regularly, and terminating or rewarding them for their performance.

All of these things must be documented—actually *written down*—if they're going to make any difference to you, your employees, your managers, or your bank account!

And then you've got to persist with that system, come hell or high water. Just as

Ray Kroc did. Just as Walt Disney did. Just as Sam Walton did.

This leads us to our next topic of discussion: the subject of estimating. But first, let's listen to what John has to say on the subject of team members. ❧

Building a Professional Team

John K. Rost

The best executive is one who has sense enough to pick good men to do what he wants done, and self-restraint enough to keep from meddling with them while they do it.

—Theodore Roosevelt

We've already taken a look at many of the matters related to associates in the chapter on Critical Staffing Decisions. We've discussed *when* to hire additional staff, *who* to hire, and *where* to find them. But it doesn't end there. So you've recruited your team. Now what?

At this point, you have to focus on an entirely new set of issues.

- Managing expectations.
- Rewarding performance.
- Ensuring employee retention.

What this all comes down to is having happy employees who reward you with attention to detail and long-term loyalty. It's all about balance, and when things go out of balance, one of you will be miserable—either you or your team.

It should be fairly obvious that the first two points will have a significant impact on the third.

Let's look at "Managing Expectations." I believe people are much happier when they know what is expected of them. These expectations must be *clearly stated, evenly applied,* and *reasonable.*

By *clearly stated,* I mean that there should be no ambiguity. And there should be no surprises. If at all possible, avoid "springing" new expectations on new team members after you've hired them.

By *evenly applied,* I mean don't play favorites. Don't give one employee the best hours, or cherry-pick clients for them. Be fair in your assignments. I realize the world generally is not "fair," but that doesn't mean you can't be.

By *reasonable,* consider taking the advice of a former boss of mine. His policy was, "I never ask any employee to do any job I wouldn't do myself."

Now let's turn to the all-important topic of "Rewarding Performance." Everyone loves rewards. In fact, too many people thrive on them. If someone exceeds expectations, or solves a problem in creative ways, that individual should be rewarded.

Rewards can take two forms: tangible and intangible.

Tangible rewards include raises, bonuses, dinner certificates, and prizes. Everyone loves those!

But intangible rewards are often as meaningful, and can include such things as public praise (in meetings), private praise, awards, badges, certificates, and so on. It's likely that, as children, we were rewarded with gold stars on our homework papers, A's, B's, or, in my case, mostly C's on our report cards, and trophies for music or sports performances. These things were important in our younger years. Don't assume that they are any less important now.

As important as it is to recognize and reward *individual* achievement, it is equally important to recognize and reward *team* performance. After a particularly good month, reward everyone with a special catered lunch, or movie tickets, or "happy hour." It doesn't have to be something big to be appreciated by your team. They just want to know that *they* and *their efforts* are appreciated!

Finally, look at "Ensuring Employee Retention."

This is an important topic because it is far less costly to make a current employee happy through managing expectations and rewarding performance than it is to seek out, interview, hire, and train new employees. So your goal must be to "keep the good ones," and, yes, "ditch the losers." I hate to put it that way, but there's no better way to look at it.

I have a friend who, on the surface, appeared to do all of this correctly. He was not in the insurance field, but he ran a somewhat similar service business. His philosophy was "reward, reward, reward." He had season tickets to everything, and gave them out liberally. In the summer, he closed his office on Friday afternoons, took them all out on his rather sizable boat, and provided mass quantities of food and drink.

He frequently took them to lunch, and threw lavish holiday parties complete with dinner, live entertainment, limo service, and overnight hotel rooms.

He provided regular raises and bonuses, promised tuition reimbursement for relevant college courses, and even offered "medical reimbursement"—cash he paid to cover deductibles and other costs not covered by his nearly almost fully-funded health insurance plan.

Did all of this achieve his intended objective? You'd think it would have, but it didn't. Since the rewards were so liberally and generally applied to everyone, the employees saw themselves as passengers on a never-ending "gravy train." His best employees valued job satisfaction more highly than parties and events, so they jumped ship and went to work for his competitors. The losers had no place to go, so they hung around and milked the system any way they could.

The big issue is that my friend had no system in place to develop top-performing employees. He had no system in place to determine what he was actually measuring and rewarding. In other words, he failed to manage expectation—something that must be considered *before* a new employee is hired, and then be viewed as an ongoing process.

Michael makes the very clear point that an Employee Development System is an action plan designed to tell you what you are looking for in a team member. It includes the "exact benchmarks, accountabilities, timing of fulfillment, and budget you will assign to the process of looking for ideal employees, identifying them, recruiting them, interviewing them, training them, managing their work, auditing their performance, compensating them, reviewing them regularly, and terminating or rewarding them for their performance."

If you plan to open and operate an independent insurance store, these are all very important considerations and cannot be left to chance. The policies and procedures must all become part of an established system—the "employee system."

As a Fiesta Auto Insurance franchisee, the process is established, tested, and proven. That all combines to create the system that enables franchisees to get off to a "running start" and begin making money almost immediately. ✤

CHAPTER

13

On the Subject of Estimating

Michael E. Gerber

The best we can do is size up the chances, calculate the risks involved, estimate our ability to deal with them, and then make our plans with confidence.

—Henry Ford

One of the greatest weaknesses of insurance store owners and managers is accurately estimating how long meetings will take and then scheduling their clients accordingly. *Webster's Collegiate Dictionary* defines *estimate* as "a rough or approximate calculation." Anyone who has visited a typical insurance store's waiting room knows that those estimates can be rough indeed.

Do you want to work with someone who gives you a rough approximation? Can you imagine making major life decisions about money or property or other important matters based solely on a rough approximation? The results wouldn't be pretty.

Do you follow this? Since entrepreneurs believe they're incapable of knowing how to organize their time, they build a business based on lack of knowing and lack of control. They build a business based on estimates.

I once had an insurance agent ask me, "What do we do when something completely unexpected happens? How can we give proper service and stay on schedule?"

The solution is interest, attention, analysis. Try detailing what you do at the beginning of an interaction, what you do in the middle, and what you do at the end.

How long does each take? In the absence of such detailed, quantified standards, everything ends up being an estimate, and a poor estimate at that.

However, an insurance store organized around a system, with adequate staff to run it, has time for proper attention. It's built right into the system.

Too many agents have grown accustomed to thinking in terms of estimates without thinking about what the term really means. Is it any wonder many insurance stores are in trouble?

Enlightened agents, in contrast, banish the word "estimate" from their vocabulary. When it comes to estimating, just say no! "But you can never be exact," agents have told me for years. "Close, maybe. But never exact."

I have a simple answer to that: you have to be. You simply can't afford to be inexact. You can't accept inexactness in yourself or in your insurance store. You can't go to work every day believing that your business, the work you do, and the commitment you make are all too complex and unpredictable to be exact. With a mind-set like that, you're doomed to run a sloppy ship. A ship that will eventually sink and suck you down with it.

This is so easy to avoid. Sloppiness—in both thought and action—is the root cause of your frustrations.

The solution to those frustrations is clarity. Clarity gives you the ability to set a clear direction, which fuels the momentum you need to grow your business.

Clarity, direction, momentum—they all come from insisting on exactness. But how do you create exactness in a hopelessly inexact world? The answer is: You discover the exactness in your business by refusing to do any work that can't be controlled exactly. The only other option is to analyze the market, determine where the opportunities are, and then organize your store to be the exact provider of the services you've chosen to offer.

Two choices and only two choices: (1) Evaluate your business and then limit yourself to the tasks you know you can do exactly, or (2) start all over by analyzing the market, identifying the key opportunities in that market, and building a business that operates exactly.

What you cannot do, what you must refuse to do, from this day forward, is to allow yourself to operate with an inexact mindset. It will lead you to ruin.

Which leads us inexorably back to the word I have been using throughout this book: Systems.

Who makes estimates? Only agents who are unclear about exactly how to do the task in question. Only agents whose experience has taught them that if something can go wrong, it will—and it'll happen to *them*!

I'm not suggesting that a systems solution will guarantee that you always perform exactly as promised. But I am saying that a systems solution will faithfully alert you when you're going off track, and will do it before you have to pay the price for it. In short, with a systems solution in place, your need to estimate will be a thing of the past, both because you have organized your business to anticipate mistakes and because you have put in place the system to do something about those mistakes before they blow up.

There is also this: to make a promise you intend to keep places a burden on you and your managers to dig deeply into how you intend to keep it. Such a burden will transform your intentions and increase your attention to detail.

With the promise will come dedication. With dedication will come integrity. With integrity will come consistency. With consistency will come results you can count on. And results you can count on mean that you get exactly what you hoped for at the outset of your business: that true pride of ownership that every insurance store owner should experience.

This brings us to the subject of clients. Who are they? Why do they come to you? How can you identify yours? And who should your clients be? But first, let's listen to what John has to say about estimating. ✤

14

There's More to Selling Than Giving a Quote

John K. Rost

There is only one way...to get anybody to do anything. And that is by making the other person want to do it.

—Dale Carnegie

While estimating the amount of time to allow for certain appointments and the completion of paperwork is of vital importance in most businesses—and even in many insurance businesses—it is less important in the management of a Fiesta Auto Insurance store. That's because at least 90% of our business is the result of walk-in traffic. People know they need automobile insurance, they see our very clear and specific outdoor signage, and they make an often sudden and impulsive decision to walk in our door and inquire.

That, of course, is when training and selling skills kick in. Through experience, we know that our presentation, along with closing the sale, writing the contract, and taking the customer's deposit will generally take about 30 to 45 minutes.

So, in terms of estimating, our issue becomes that of scheduling an adequate number of agents to handle clients during our relatively predictable rush times. We've discovered that the worst thing we can do is keep a potential client waiting for a long time to be served.

In our business, clients are not usually in our offices because they "want" to buy auto insurance. They're there because they "have" to buy it. So we focus on matching their specific needs with the most appropriate carrier (in terms of coverage, cost, and value), and then we provide a quote. They may not necessarily be focused on price alone: they are savvy buyers.

That's why the quote is more than simply price. In fact, if a potential client walks in and asks for a quote and we give it to him or her without making it part of our total selling process, chances are that customer will say something like, "Let me think about it and I'll get back you." Of course, in most cases, they won't get back to us.

That's why we make sure that the customer gets engaged in the total process of purchasing auto insurance. In marketing terms, we want to reach both the conscious mind and the unconscious mind. We want to make certain that on all levels the customer has positive feelings about the process. What do they see around them when they walk in? How are they greeted? How are they treated? If they have kids, how are the kids treated? In other words, you must create a system for giving a quote—from that first greeting to the collection of money to the processing of the documents. I referred to this earlier as our 'selling system."

Here are a couple of examples of our selling system. By consistently applying them, we are able to accurately estimate the length of each appointment as well as our closing percentage.

First, when a potential customer walks in the door, the agent on duty (if available) should stand up and walk toward the customer and greet her. Even if the agent and customer are only separated by three or four feet, the agent should walk toward the customer, shake hands, say, "Hi, how are you?" and establish eye contact.

The successful insurance professional does not remain seated at the desk, wave the customer over and say, "Come have a seat here." We estimate that this part of the selling process takes less than one minute, including all of the necessary introductions.

Second, the agent will walk over to the refrigerator, grab an ice cold Coke, open it, and hand it to the customer. We don't ask the customer if she wants something to drink. Most people, because they just walked in and they don't want to get into a situation where now they're going to be forced to buy something, will just naturally say, "No." That's the typical response.

We know that if a person is already feeling a little bit uncomfortable—because nobody likes to be sold and no one really likes buying insurance—she will be sitting back defensively with arms folded, but if we can get a Coke in her hand, now all of a sudden her arms aren't going to be folded. So her body language and posture are going to relax. There's also that subconscious thought: "The agent gave me something without even asking."

New franchisees in training sometimes ask me, "Why don't you offer a bottle of water?" While a bottle of water is fine to a certain degree, it's not going to have the same impact a Coke will have. The moment somebody touches a cold Coke can, it's going to send certain signals to their body that will help wake them up.

A cold bottle of water will do the same thing, of course, but the next thing that happens when the customer takes a sip is that her body is going to wake up even more, because she will have sugar and caffeine kicking in over the next five or ten minutes, during the period when we're going through the quoting process. The client is actually starting to feel more alive—she'll have more energy.

If you're dealing with a customer who has her hands open, is touching a cold drink, and is taking in sugar and caffeine, she's starting to feel better. The subconscious mind is telling her, "Wow, I'm just feeling better, this is good. Okay, let's go ahead and write that policy I need today."

Now, if you give the customer a Coke and the response is, "I don't drink Coke. Do you happen to have a bottle of water?" then go ahead and offer her water. But if you start off by asking, "Would you like a Coke or a bottle of water?" most people are going to say no and sit there with arms folded. That means you've missed out on the opportunity to get them to open up.

This strategy costs you hardly anything, but if you don't follow that aspect of the selling system in exactly that order—if you get lazy—then it doesn't have the intended outcome of your customer physically and emotionally starting to feel better.

This aspect takes no more than two or three minutes. And I've discovered that the superstars really "get it" and do it without fail.

The next part of our selling system (something you can replicate) is our short, engaging video that is presented on an iPad, in the customer's choice of either English or Spanish. While the customer is watching, our superstars are watching with them. The non-stars turn away and work on their computers—a subtle clue that the video really isn't important. Our selling system involves staying connected throughout the entire meeting. The video is only three and a half minutes in length, but it is both powerful and essential.

There are several steps in the system after the video ends. The bottom line is that everything is designed and structured to turn the prospect into an actual customer.

After the transaction is completed, the superstars always walk the customer out to the car and shake hands again. They don't simply say goodbye and move on to the next task. A customer's car could be one of the most expensive investments he or she has ever made, so naturally both pride and joy are invested in that car. If it's a car they just bought, they're not going to simply drive it home and park it. No, they're thinking about showing it off…maybe taking family or friends for a ride. Our superstars cement the relationship by expressing interest in their clients and their cars.

We know from experience that this entire process takes from 30 to 45 minutes. So we know that we can tell the next customer who walks in how soon we will be able to help them. Our goal, however, is to cut wait time down to a minimum—five minutes or less. This can be done by having adequate staff on hand during peak times, and by moving the process along by carefully planning and controlling every key aspect of it.

This is our selling system in a nutshell. It isn't the entire plan, of course, but these are the basics.

To make sure the process goes smoothly with a minimum of interruption, we take it one step further. Each of the desks in our offices is L-shaped, and on the smaller part of the L, we place an inexpensive multi-function office device: a printer/scanner/copier/fax machine. Every desk, meaning every agent, of course, has one.

There are three key advantages to equipping our agents this way, rather than using a single centralized printer in the back office. First, the agent doesn't have to get up from his or her desk to complete the transaction. That saves time and keeps the attention focused on the customer. Second, a centralized machine can get "backed up" if more than one agent has to use it. And finally, if one machine breaks or runs out of toner, another machine on a nearby desk can serve as a backup. These devices have gotten to be so inexpensive that there is no real reason not to equip every agent with one.

Some agencies still operate under the "old school" system of paper, manila folders, and file cabinets. But with today's computerized agency management systems, the need to get up, walk over to the file cabinet, and retrieve a file is eliminated. It's so much better to be able to scan documents, make copies for the customer, and retrieve all the information you need with just a few keystrokes...all without leaving your desk. And with today's "cloud" technology for backing up your files, there is no fear of losing everything through a hard drive crash!

Systems and technology have merged in amazing ways to make the process of writing insurance policies more streamlined than we ever imagined ten or twenty years ago. But always remember that—whether using paper files or computers, scanners, and copiers—your selling system has to be at the heart of your insurance store. Now let's see what revelations Michael has in store for us as he discusses the subject of clients. ❧

CHAPTER
15

On the Subject of Clients

Michael E. Gerber

I don't build in order to have clients. I have clients in order to build
—Ayn Rand

When it comes to the insurance business, the best definition of clients I've ever heard is this: **Clients: Very special people who drive most agents crazy.** Does that work for you?

After all, it's a rare client who shows any appreciation for what an agent has to go through to get the best rates—especially when there are problems with a client's insurability. Don't they always think the premiums are too high? And don't they focus on problems rather than on all the times you bend over backward to give them what they need?

Do you ever hear your employees voice these complaints? More to the point, have you ever voiced them yourself? Well, you're not alone. I have yet to meet an agent who doesn't suffer from a strong case of client confusion. Client confusion is about:

- what your client really wants;
- how to communicate effectively with your client;
- how to keep your client happy;
- how to deal with client dissatisfaction; and
- whom to call a client.

Confusion 1: What Does Your Client Really Want?

Your clients aren't just people; they're very specific kinds of people. Let me share with you the six categories of clients as seen from the E-Myth marketing perspective: (1) tactile clients, (2) neutral clients, (3) withdrawal clients, (4) experimental clients, (5) transitional clients, and (6) traditional clients.

Your entire marketing strategy must be based on which type of client you are dealing with. Each of the six client types spends money on insurance for very different, and identifiable, reasons. These are:

- Tactile clients get their major gratification from interacting with other people.
- Neutral clients get their major gratification from interacting with inanimate objects (a computer, a car, information).
- Withdrawal clients get their major gratification from interacting with ideas (thoughts, concepts, stories).
- Experimental clients rationalize their buying decisions by perceiving that what they bought is new, revolutionary, and innovative.
- Transitional clients rationalize their buying decisions by perceiving that what they bought is dependable and reliable.
- Traditional clients rationalize their buying decisions by perceiving that what they bought is cost-effective, a good deal, and worth the money.

  In short:
  - If your clients are tactile, you have to emphasize the *people* of your store.

- If your clients are neutral, you have to emphasize the *technology* of your store.
- If your clients are withdrawal clients, you have to emphasize the *idea* of your store.
- If your clients are experimental clients, you have to emphasize the *uniqueness* of your store.
- If your clients are transitional, you have to emphasize the *dependability* of your company and the insurance providers you represent.
- If your clients are traditional, you have to talk about the *financial competitiveness* of your store.

What your clients want is determined by who they are. Who they are is regularly demonstrated by what they do. Think about the clients with whom you do business. Ask yourself: In which of the categories would I place them? What do they do for a living?

If you're working with a mechanic, for example, it's probably safe to assume he's a neutral client. If another one of your clients is a teacher, she's probably tactile. Accountants tend to be traditional, and people in the computer field are often experimental.

Having an idea about which categories your clients may fall into is very helpful to figuring out what they want. Of course there's no exact science to it, and human beings constantly defy stereotypes. So don't take my word for it. You'll want to make your own analysis of the clients you serve.

Confusion 2: How to Communicate Effectively with Your Clients

The next step in the client satisfaction process is to decide how to magnify the characteristics of your business that are most likely to appeal to your preferred category of client. That begins with what marketing people call your positioning strategy.

What do I mean by *positioning* your business? You position your store with words—a few well-chosen words to tell your clients exactly what they want to hear. In marketing lingo, those words are called your USP, or unique selling proposition.

For example, if you are targeting tactile clients (ones who love people), your USP could be: "Where the feelings of people *really* count!" If you are targeting experimental clients (ones who love new, revolutionary things), your USP could be: "Where living on the edge is a way of life!" In other words, when they choose to buy from your store, they can count on your services being unique, original, and on the cutting edge.

Is this starting to make sense? Do you see how the ordinary things most insurance agents do to get clients can be done in a significantly more effective way?

Once you understand the essential principles of marketing the E-Myth Way, the strategies by which you attract clients can make an enormous difference in your market share.

Confusion 3: How to Keep Your Clients Happy

Let's say you've overcome the first two confusions. Great. Now how do you keep your client happy?

Very simple…just keep your promise! And make sure your client *knows* you kept your promise every step of the way.

In short, giving your clients what they think they want is the key to keeping your clients (or anyone else, for that matter) really happy.

If your clients need to interact with people (high touch, tactile), make certain that they do.

If they need to interact with things (high-tech, neutral), make certain that they do.

If they need to interact with ideas (in their head, withdrawal), make certain that they do.

And so forth.

At E-Myth, we call this your client fulfillment system. It's the step-by-step process by which you do the task you've contracted to do and deliver what you've promised—on time, every time.

But what happens when your clients are *not* happy? What happens when you've done everything I've mentioned here and your client is still dissatisfied?

Confusion 4: How to Deal with Client Dissatisfaction

If you have followed each step up to this point, client dissatisfaction will be rare. But it can and will still occur—people are people, and some people will always find a way to be dissatisfied with something. Here's what to do about it:

- Always listen to what your clients are saying. And never interrupt while they're saying it.
- After you're sure you've heard all of your client's complaint, make absolutely certain you understand what she said by phrasing a question such as: "Can I repeat what you've just told me to make absolutely certain I understand you?"
- Secure your client's acknowledgement that you have heard her complaint accurately.
- Apologize for whatever your client thinks you did that dissatisfied her…even if you didn't do it!
- After your client has acknowledged your apology, ask her exactly what would make her happy.
- Repeat what your client told you would make her happy, and get her acknowledgement that you have heard correctly.
- If at all possible, give your client exactly what she has asked for.

You may be thinking, "But what if my client wants something totally impossible?"

Don't worry. If you've followed my recommendations to the letter, what your client asks for will seldom seem unreasonable.

Confusion 5: Whom to Call Clients

At this stage, it's important to ask yourself some questions about the kind of clients you hope to attract to your insurance store:

- Which types of clients would you most like to do business with?
- Where do you see your real market opportunities?
- Who would you like to work with, provide insurance to, and position your business for?

To what category of client are you most drawn? A tactile client, for whom people are most important? A neutral client, for whom the mechanics of how you present policy options is most important? An experimental client, for whom cutting-edge innovation is important? Or a traditional client, for whom low cost and certainty of delivery are absolutely essential?

Once you've defined your ideal clients, go after them. There's no reason you can't attract these types of people to your insurance store and give them exactly what they want.

In short, *it's all up to you*. No mystery. No magic. Just a systematic process for shaping your business's future. But you must have the passion to pursue the process. And you must be absolutely clear about every aspect of it.

Until you know your clients as well as you know yourself.

Until all your complaints about clients are a thing of the past.

Until you accept the undeniable fact that client acquisition and client satisfaction are more science than art.

But unless you're willing to grow your business, you better not follow any of these recommendations. Because if you do what I'm suggesting, it's going to grow.

This brings us to the subject of *growth*. But first, let's listen to what John has to say about clients. ❧

Making It All About the Customer

John K. Rost

*The glue that holds all relationships together—including the relationship
between the leader and the led, is trust. And trust is based on integrity.*
—Brian Tracy

While customers can sometimes cause stress—especially
when they miss a monthly payment and we have to find
them and reinstate their policies—for the most part, we
LOVE our customers!

Our customers are everything to us. Without customers there is no
business. Clients depend on us to give them what they know they need
and, more importantly, to effectively offer them what they didn't know
they might need. Our job is to advise and ultimately protect a client
from possible disaster.

After all, that's the definition of insurance. *Webster's Dictionary* says that
insurance is a system of protection against loss. Our job is to help protect our
customers with products that insure their vehicles, homes, and businesses.

With the advent of easy-to-use computer programs, many agents do not think of their customers as special people with specific needs. Instead, they start filling out a form on the computer. After a few minutes of these back and forth questions and answers, the computer spits out a quote. The agent then sits back and hopes that this is the cheapest rate ever quoted to the customer and the customer agrees to buy.

Is this you? I hope not, but it was me—and most likely every agent at one time. It is an easy trap to fall into. Do your best when engaging with customers to mix things up a bit. Ask questions not listed in the rating program.

I suggest you create ten of these questions and ask at least five of the given ten. Some of these questions could be: When was the last time you purchased insurance? Was this purchase for the same car that you have today? How long have you lived in the area? What kind of work do you do? Do you have family in the area? Last time you purchased insurance do you remember what the down payment was? What was your previous monthly payment? Was it for this vehicle or a different one? These are just simple examples, but they serve the purpose of providing you with valuable information, and they create conversation points.

As you know, a fundamental truth about selling is that people want to buy from people they like. Price isn't everything. Service is. Simple things like creating laughter and warm dialogue with the customer help build rapport. Focus on building a system that creates great customer rapport and price will diminish in importance to the customer.

Every day, ask yourself, "Is my business really all about the customer?" Try your best to distance yourself from the agency and view it from a client's perspective. Did you create the floor plan of the store to accommodate the needs of the customer, or to make you, the owner, feel good?

When coaching our franchisees, I commonly remind them to ask this question anytime they want to change any aspect of the Fiesta system: "Are you doing this for yourself or for the customer?"

Invariably what they want to do is for their own benefit as the owner and not for the customer.

Here's an example: I know an agency owner who was so frustrated by customers' children running around in the office that he moved the furniture of the store in order to eliminate room to run.

What he really did was create a space that looked unsightly and disorganized. At the core of this issue is the fact that kids are obviously important to every customer who walks in the door with them. To make the customer happy (and feel important), it might be a good idea to make the customer's kids happy (and feel important).

I suggested that he create a kids' corner where children can have coloring books or other toys to play with at a table built for kids. At Fiesta, we took it a step further and created a wall mural of "Max," our mascot, along with cartoon kids. (More on Max in a few pages.) The caption on the mural reads: "Max's Kids' Club."

When an owner incorporates this into his or her store, kids quite naturally run to this section. Now the kids are occupied and the owner has sent a positive message to a customer: "We care about your children." And now he has the opportunity to pursue the sale. Two ways to solve a problem—one is negative and one is positive.

How about the personality of you and your agents?

I recall an agent who became a franchisee. As he took on the challenges of ownership, he refused to continue to grow as an individual. Instead he approached challenges with depression and every customer was an opportunity to dump his troubles in their laps.

Have you ever experienced this kind of behavior by a sales person? Price won't matter to the customer, because he simply doesn't want to hear someone else's problems and will take his business elsewhere. It's much easier for positive and happy people to create conversation with customers and build rapport. Focus all of your energy in building your business on providing for the customer's needs with value and service. It's your job as an owner to cultivate this type of atmosphere and lead your staff.

When potential customers walk through your door, they should feel like the most important people on earth. In reality, they are! Treat them right, treat their kids right, and you will have loyal customers for life! ✤

CHAPTER

17

On the Subject of Growth

Michael E. Gerber

*As we learn we always change, and so our perception. This changed
perception then becomes a new Teacher inside each of us.*

—Hyemeyohsts Storm

The rule of business growth says that every business, like every
child, is destined to grow. Needs to grow. Is determined
to grow.

Once you've created your business, once you've shaped the idea
of it, the most natural thing for it to do is to...*grow*! And if you stop
it from growing, it will die.

It falls squarely on the insurance store owner to help it grow. To
nurture it and support it in every way. To infuse it with these qualities:

- purpose;
- passion;
- will;

- belief;
- personality; and
- method.

As your business grows, it naturally changes. And as it changes from a little business to something much bigger, you will begin to feel out of control. And that's because you are out of control!

Your business has exceeded your know-how, sprinted right past you, and now it's taunting you to keep up. That leaves you two choices: grow as big as your business demands you to grow, or try to hold your business at its present level—at the level you feel most comfortable.

The sad fact is that most owners do the latter. They try to keep their businesses small, securely within their comfort zone. Doing what they know how to do, what they feel most comfortable doing. It's called playing it safe.

But as the business grows, the number, scale, and complexity of tasks will grow, too, until they threaten to overwhelm the owner. More people are needed. More space. More money. Everything seems to be happening at the same time. A hundred balls are in the air at once.

As I've said throughout this book: Most insurance store owners are not entrepreneurs. They aren't true businesspeople at all, but technicians suffering from an entrepreneurial seizure. Their philosophy of coping with the workload can be summarized as "just do it," rather than figuring out how to get it done through other people using innovative systems to produce consistent results.

Given most owners' inclination to be the master juggler in their business, it's not surprising that as complexity increases, as work expands beyond their ability to do it, as money becomes more elusive, they are just holding on, desperately juggling more and more balls. In the end, most collapse under the strain.

You can't expect your business to stand still. You can't expect your business to stay small. A business that stays small and depends on you to do everything isn't a business—it's a job!

Yes, just like your children, your business must be allowed to grow, to flourish, to change, to become more than it is. In this way, it will match your vision.

Do you feel the excitement? You should. After all, you know what your business *is*, but not what it *can be*.

It's either going to grow or die. The choice is yours, but it is a choice that must be made. If you sit back and wait for change to overtake you, you will always have to answer no to this question: Are you ready?

This brings us to the subject of *change*. But first, let's listen to what John has to say about growth. ✤

When and Why Two or More Are Better

John K. Rost

If you don't know where you're going, you'll probably end up somewhere else.

—Yogi Berra

I f your goal in opening your insurance store is to work *in* your business rather than *on* your business, welcome to your new job. You can likely count on working long hours for the rest of your life.

But if your goal is to grow an enterprise, I believe there are three essential things you must do:

- Position the business,
- Market the business, and
- Replicate the business.

By "position the business," I mean decide what you want to offer to what market(s), and then open the business in an appropriate location and give it a meaningful name.

By "market the business," I mean use those tools that will reach your target market as efficiently (cost-effectively) as possible.

By "replicate the business," I mean use the systems you have implemented to add additional locations—to open new stores that will essentially "run themselves" so you can enjoy your life. Don't laugh…this actually works!

It really doesn't matter if you intend to grow your "mom-and-pop" insurance store or if you choose to become part of another organization; these principles are universal. They apply in either case. In fact, if you want to grow your own enterprise, they apply even more directly to you, because in most franchise situations, nearly everything is established and field-proven.

Position the Business

It sounds simple on the surface, but what you name your insurance store will have an impact on your success. Your name should not only attract customers, but it should inform your target market that you are there for them, specifically. As I pointed out earlier, putting a sign above your door that simply says "Insurance" does not distinguish you in any way. If you are going to successfully apply Michael's principles of Purpose, Passion, Will, Belief, Personality, and Method to your business in order to grow, setting yourself apart through your name is very important.

Through the years I have had many discussions about our name and why it begins with the word "Fiesta." Fiesta Auto Insurance sounds ridiculous to some people, because they think we are saying "Party Auto Insurance."

When I started the company, I made the conscious decision that I was going to position the company to pursue a specific group of customers. I knew that my niche could be one that was often overlooked by others—to their detriment.

The focus of Fiesta Auto Insurance therefore became the Hispanic and Latin consumer. (Typically, Hispanic refers to someone with Mexican heritage, and Latin refers to someone with roots in another Spanish-speaking country.)

I had the opportunity to work with this group of consumers early on and noticed certain characteristics that I really liked. For instance, Hispanic and Latin consumers still prefer to deal face-to-face when buying insurance. In addition, when they find a home for their insurance and are happy with the service, they share this information with family and friends. It is much more likely for Hispanic or Latin consumers to ask a friend or family member for a referral to buy insurance than to open the Yellow Pages or refer to some other form of advertisement. And when they get a positive referral, they are very likely to buy.

I then looked at income levels and realized that some (but not all) of the consumers in this market would likely be considered "non-standard," as opposed to the "standard" or preferred consumer.

The so-called preferred customer tends to be more affluent, which generally means that they are more likely to buy direct or by mail, using a credit card in a transaction that does not require direct contact with a licensed agent. This customer is also more likely to have less loyalty to the agent as they really do not need face-to-face contact. How often does a preferred client really talk with an Allstate, Farmers, or State Farm agent? They can simply call an 800 number to add a vehicle or make a payment.

Our non-standard customer has different needs—needs that I believe create rapport and increase loyalty. Most clients in this category prefer to deal face-to-face when buying an insurance policy. In our case, the customer is able to walk in and sit down in a friendly, well-branded insurance store where the agent can also converse in Spanish. While many customers who are Spanish-speaking are fully bilingual, they often prefer to speak in Spanish when possible. The agent's ability to speak Spanish creates a bond that is unique to our stores.

Having an insurance store name that starts with Fiesta sends a signal to our consumer that they most likely will be able to communicate with the agent in Spanish. At the same time, the word "Fiesta" is almost universal in acceptance. Most English-only consumers don't realize that when they refer to the city of Los Angeles, they are speaking Spanish words that mean "The Angels." It is simply "Los Angeles" and not thought of as Spanish. This is true for Fiesta. Most English speakers think of the word as a friendly lighthearted name that simply precedes the description of the product we sell—Auto Insurance. At Fiesta Auto Insurance there is no doubt to the consumer who we are and what we offer.

Of course, where the store is located is of prime importance. You want to set up shop in the area where your target customers and people like them do their shopping, find their entertainment, service their cars, attend their places of worship, and enroll their kids in school. Obviously, then, we don't open our stores in areas surrounded by gated communities with multi-million-dollar homes. Yes, there are Hispanics who live in gated communities in luxurious homes. But they likely won't become our customers, and what matters most is a heavy concentration of like-minded people with similar life stories.

Once our customer is in the office, our agents have the opportunity to discuss other insurance needs: homes, recreational vehicles, commercial vehicles, and businesses. We do much more than just write auto insurance. However, vehicle liability insurance is mandatory in almost every state, whereas other insurance coverage is not required by law.

If you plan to open your own store, your name—if possible—should reference the products you are offering or the market you intend to reach. If you create a name that is too broad or not identified with a specific product, there could be challenges. AFLAC spent tens of millions in advertising to explain the nature of their business product. That's a luxury few, if any of us, will have.

Market the Business

I promised you that I would talk about "Max," our mascot. Max is one of the key ways we attract customers into our stores. Yes, we use radio, television, and newspapers (especially Spanish-market ones), but one of our most effective means of bringing in our target customers is Max, a lovable, animated bird. Actually, Max is a loveable, animated person inside a bird costume! (Think Ronald McDonald.)

I recall visiting one of our franchisees in Florida who, within just a few weeks of opening his store, had hit a soaring home run. In fact, it was a grand slam homer! He was reporting sales numbers in his first and second month that we normally expect to see in five or six months. So I asked him how he was doing it.

"Well, someone from the newspaper drove by and saw Max standing out front waving at passing cars. He decided he liked the gimmick, so he took pictures and ran them in the paper. Not only that, but he posted it online. Underneath the posting, a customer added a note that said, 'This is the real deal. This is a great place to go for insurance. When I went in, they promptly gave me a drink, seated me, and it was an easy process.'"

Always a little suspicious, I asked the owner, "Did you guys post that about yourselves or was that really a customer?" He said, "You know, I didn't even know this had been written, but it really was from a customer."

All because of a colorful bird named Max. Or, rather, someone paid to walk around in a costume and act like a bird! It's clear, then, that marketing to new customers is a key element of growth.

Once your customer walks out your door, the next phase of your program of growth through marketing must kick in. The essentials are retention of customers and referrals. A sound marketing plan must have systems to cover these areas in order to grow.

Outstanding service and follow-through are vital to retention. How quickly do you answer the phone? Does your staff return phone calls promptly? Is there a program to follow up on underwriting concerns from the carriers? Is there a clear path to reinstating policies in cases where the customer may have missed a payment? We can retain customers if we truly honor them and meet their needs!

Next, do you have a system for referrals? In those states where fee income applies, you may be able to reward a referral with cash or some other gift. Be sure to check state laws, as some do not allow a gift to a non-agent.

I have seen a clever agent write a contract and ask the client if the service and price were satisfactory. When the customer said, "Yes," the agent, very respectfully and with a smile on her face, said, "Would you mind taking a look on your cell phone and giving me the names and numbers of the last three friends you called? I'd like to call them and introduce myself as someone who could help them." Now *that* is selling!

There's much more to a good marketing tool-kit than Max waving at traffic, however. How will you use radio, TV, or print in your area? How will you differentiate yourself from your competition?

First, make sure you advertise on those stations and in those publications that reach your target market. It's often easy to buy into a salesperson's pitch based on price alone. There are inexpensive commercials available to radio and TV, but their cost is always based on size of audience and time of day (or popularity of a specific program). Responsible media salespeople will show you unbiased research that was done by outside firms in order to back up their claims. Sometimes, the task of interpreting these numbers can be challenging, so hope and pray that you work with someone who will explain it all, rather than someone who is simply trying to close the sale. Learn what the numbers mean and make good advertising *decisions*, not *guesses*.

Second, make sure that all of your advertising has a call to action. A call to action is the gimmick or coupon offered.

Third, make sure that you have a way to measure and verify the effectiveness of the promotion. Whatever tools you use, the outcome must be monitored with real numbers to gauge its effectiveness and avoid wasting money. You can't just say, "I think it worked."

Specifically, how many more policies were sold when the advertisement hit the public? How many more phone calls were received that week? Of course, if prospects stream in your door when Max is out there waving his arms, you get instant verification of the success of one part of the marketing formula!

Replicate the Business

Whether you open your own independent insurance store or you become a franchisee of a larger company, you must realize from the beginning that it's not only about growth in policies. It's all about growth in the number of locations you open. You will never become the freedom-giving enterprise you want to be with just a single location.

Fortunately for our franchisees, we have figured out all the matters related to timing, so they know when the time is right to open a second, or third, or fourth store. If you have opened—or are planning to open—your own independent store, carefully consider these guidelines.

Our plan has specific sales targets for the first six months of operation of each new store. Ultimately, I want our franchisees to own at least three locations. I know from experience that it takes three locations to truly experience dramatic increase in income, as well as freedom from being a technician. It's impossible to operate three locations as a technician, so our franchisee is strongly encouraged to think about growth from the beginning. A new franchisee should plan on having three locations in thirty-six months. If you are an independent, that should be your goal for the next three years, as well.

There are three major advantages to having multiple locations:

- You can spread marketing costs over all of them, making your investment in advertising more efficient;
- You can share staff instead of panicking when an agent calls in sick or goes on vacation; and
- You can secure a more amazing retirement than you ever imagined possible!

First, let's look at advertising and marketing. If you have one location, every dollar you invest in marketing benefits only that location. If you have three or more stores, that investment can benefit all three or more. It costs the same for a radio or TV commercial, or a print ad, or a billboard if you list only one location, or if you list three.

Next, let's consider sharing staff. The one constant in life is that it changes, often unexpectedly. Someone, someday, is going to call in sick. Or there will be a loss in the family. And that agent won't report to work. If you have multiple agents working multiple locations (especially if they are adequately cross-trained), you will be able to quickly shift an agent from a less busy location to the location that needs immediate help. Think about it: that's why NFL teams have backup quarterbacks. There has to be someone to take the ball when injury strikes.

Finally, think about your ultimate dream! No matter how much you love the insurance business and enjoy and value your customers, you probably don't want to be doing this for the rest of your life. You want to retire. Travel. Buy a boat or an RV. Enjoy the fruits of your enterprise-building activities before you end up in some nursing home. (Sorry, just telling you like it is...or could be.)

This is where the principle of EQUITY comes into play. If you've built it correctly, you can sell it.

I know of agents who have sold their stores for one million dollars, two million dollars, or more. If you think that you could retire comfortably on that amount, think about how you could live on three million, six million, or more. And think about how much more your stores would be worth to a buyer who understood the principles of shared marketing and shared staff. Welcome to your private island in the South Pacific!

Now, very honestly, opening three or more locations is not the answer if it's done incorrectly. I have one franchisee that opened his first store in San Diego, but then wanted to open his second store in Los Angeles and his third in Las Vegas. He thought that would make him the supreme ruler of a vast insurance empire.

"Not so," I advised him. "If you own stores in three different cities, you will have to buy advertising in three different cities. That's not at all efficient. And how on earth are you going to share staff when someone calls in sick...or dead? They're separated by hundreds of miles."

"So, what are you saying?" he asked.

I responded, "What I'm saying is: stick with this market. You already have a store in the San Diego area. Think about a store in El Cajon (a nearby suburb), or Ramona, at worst (a little further out). That way you can maximize your ad bucks, and maximize the cross-utilization of your time and your team's time."

I'm happy to report that "Max" came through for us all again! Our franchisee is an intelligent guy who decided that MAXimizing his advertising and MAXimizing his team really was the way to go!

You might guess that we carefully protect our territories so that our franchisees can grow their businesses into enterprises without facing internal competition. True, this may slow our growth a bit, but our franchisees are as important to us as their customers are to them.

The bottom line on all of this? If you secure your future, you also have a sense of security today. You position yourself for success so you don't have to worry about a tire blowing out. You can afford to buy new tires when they need to be replaced, thereby avoiding a disaster. When your car doesn't work properly, you have the money to drive it to the automotive shop, leave it with the mechanic, and get it repaired. When gas prices are going up dramatically, you can still fill your tank and not tell your kids, "We really can't go drive to see Grandma and Grandpa, because it's going to cost seventy-five dollars in gas, and Mom and Dad don't have that kind of money."

Life's problems are still problems, and many of them are still going to cost you money. But by building your insurance business into an enterprise, you will have the resources to deal with the unexpected.

My dream is to stand one day before 600 or 800 or 1,200 successful franchisees, all earning at least a hundred thousand dollars a year, and tell them, "We did it! We worked together! We built systems and used systems. You applied E-Myth principles to your business and grew it into an enterprise."

Wouldn't it be wonderful if you were in that audience? Imagine that! Let's see what Michael has to say about the six-letter word, CHANGE. ❧

On the Subject of Change

Michael E. Gerber

The "rest of the world" does not sit idly "out there." It is a sparkling realm of continual creation, transformation, and annihilation.
—Gary Zukav, THE DANCING WU LI MASTERS

S o your business is growing. That means, of course, that it's also changing. Which means it's driving you and everyone in your life crazy.

That's because, to most people, change is a diabolical thing. Tell most people they've got to change, and they will crawl into a shell. Nothing threatens their existence more than change. Nothing cements their resistance more than change. Nothing.

Yet for the past thirty-seven years, that's exactly what I've been proposing to small business owners: the need to change. Not for the sake of change, but for the sake of their lives.

I've talked to countless entrepreneurs whose hopes weren't being realized through their businesses; whose lives were consumed by work; who slaved increasingly longer hours for decreasing pay; whose dissatisfaction grew as their enjoyment shriveled; whose insurance business had become the worst job in the world; whose money was out of control; whose employees, both agents and support staff, were a source of never-ending hassles, just like their clients, their bank, and, increasingly, even their family.

More and more, these owners spent their time alone, dreading the unknown and anxious about their future. And even when they were with people, they didn't know how to relax. Their mind was always on the job. They were distracted by work. By the thought of work. By the fear of falling behind.

And yet, when confronted with their condition and offered an alternative, most of the same owners strenuously resisted. They assumed that if there were a better way of doing business, they already would have figured it out. They derived comfort from what they believed they already knew. They accepted the limitations of being in the insurance business; or the truth about people; or the limitations of what they could expect from their clients, their employees, their bankers— even their family and friends.

In short, most owners I've met over the years would rather live with the frustrations they already have than risk enduring new frustrations.

Isn't that true of most people you know? Rather than opening themselves up to the infinite number of possibilities life offers, they prefer to shut their life down to respectable limits. After all, isn't that the most reasonable way to live?

I think not. I think we must learn to let go. I think that if you fail to embrace change, it will inevitably destroy you.

Conversely, by opening yourself to change, you give your business the opportunity to get the most from your talents.

Let me share with you an original way to think about change, about life, about who we are and what we do. About the stunning notion of expansion and contraction.

Contraction vs. Expansion

"Our salvation," a wise man once said, "is to allow." That is, to be open, to let go of our beliefs, to change. Only then can we move from a point of view to a viewing point.

That wise man was Thaddeus Golas, the author of a small, powerful book entitled *The Lazy Man's Guide to Enlightenment* (Seed Center, 1971). Among the many inspirational things he had to say was this compelling idea:

> *The basic function of each being is expanding and contracting. Expanded beings are permeable; contracted beings are dense and impermeable. Therefore each of us, alone or in combination, may appear as space, energy, or mass, depending on the ration of expansion to contraction chosen, and what kind of vibrations each of us expresses by alternating expansion and contraction. Each being controls his own vibrations.*

In other words, Golas tells us that the entire mystery of life can be summed up in two words: *expansion* and *contraction*. He goes on to say:

> *We experience expansion as awareness, comprehension, understanding, or whatever we wish to call it.*
>
> *When we are completely expanded, we have a feeling of total awareness, of being one with all life.*
>
> *At that level we have no resistance to any vibrations or inter-actions with other beings. It is timeless bliss, with unlimited choice of consciousness, perception, and feeling.*
>
> *On the other hand, when a (human) being is totally contracted, he is a mass particle, completely imploded.*
>
> *To the degree that he is contracted, a being is unable to be in the same space with others, so contraction is felt as fear, pain, unconsciousness, ignorance, hatred, evil, and a whole host of strange feelings.*

> *At an extreme of contraction, a human being has the feeling*
> *of being completely insane, of resisting everyone and every-*
> *thing, of being unable to choose the content of his consciousness.*
>   *Of course, these are just the feelings appropriate to mass vibra-*
> *tion levels, and he can get out of them at any time by expanding,*
> *by letting go of all resistance to what he thinks, sees, or feels."*

Stay with me here. Because what Golas says is profoundly important. When you're feeling oppressed, overwhelmed, exhausted by
more than you can control—contracted, as Golas puts it—you can
change your state to one of expansion.

According to Golas, the more contracted we are, the more threatened by change; the more expanded we are, the more open to change.

In our most enlightened—that is, open—state, change is as
welcome as non-change. Everything is perceived as a part of ourselves.
There is no inside or outside. Everything is one thing. Our sense of
isolation is transformed to a feeling of ease, of light, of a joyful relationship with everything.

As infants, we didn't even think of change in the same way,
because we lived those first days in an unthreatened state. Insensitive
to the threat of loss, most young children are only aware of *what is.*
Change is simply another form of *what is.* Change just *is.*

However, when we are in our most contracted—that is, closed—
state, change is the most extreme threat. If the known is what I have, then
the unknown must be what threatens to take away what I have. Change,
then, is the unknown. And the unknown is fear. It's like being
between trapezes.

- To the fearful, change is threatening because things may get worse.
- To the hopeful, change is encouraging because things may
  get better.
- To the confident, change is inspiring because the challenge
  exists to improve things.

If you are fearful, you see difficulties in every opportunity. If you
are fear-free, you see opportunities in every difficulty. Fear protects

what I have from being taken away. But it also disconnects me from the rest of the world. In other words, fear keeps me separate and alone.

Here's the exciting part of Golas's message: With this new understanding of contraction and expansion, we can become completely attuned to where we are at all times.

If I am afraid, suspicious, skeptical, and resistant, I am in a contracted state. If I am joyful, open, interested, and willing, I am in an expanded state. Just knowing this puts me on an expanded path. Always remembering this, Golas assures us, brings enlightenment, which opens me even more.

Such openness gives me the ability to freely access my options. And taking advantage of options is the best part of change. If you believe Thaddeus Golas, your most exciting option is to be open to all of them.

Because your life is lived on a continuum between the most contracted and most expanded—the most closed and most open—states, change is best understood as the movement from one to the other, and back again.

Most small business owners I've met see change as a thing-in-itself, as something that just happens to them. Most experience change as a threat. Whenever change shows up at the door, they quickly slam it. Many bolt the door and pile up the furniture. Some even run for their gun.

Few of them understand that change isn't a thing-in-itself, but rather the manifestation of many things. You might call it the revelation of all possibilities. Think of it as the ability at any moment to sacrifice what we are for what we could become.

Change can either challenge us or threaten us. It's our choice. Our attitude toward change can either pave the way to success or throw up a roadblock. Change is where opportunity lives. Without change we would stay exactly as we are. The universe would be frozen still. Time would end.

At any given moment, we are somewhere on the path between a contracted and expanded state. Most of us are in the middle of the journey, neither totally closed nor totally open. According to Golas, change is our movement from one place in the middle toward one of the two ends.

Do you want to move toward contraction or toward enlighten-ment? Because without change, you are hopelessly stuck with what you've got.

Without change:

- we have no hope;
- we cannot know true joy;
- we will not get better; and
- we will continue to focus exclusively on what we have and the threat of losing it.

All of this negativity contracts us even more, until, at the extreme closed end of the spectrum, we become a black hole so dense that no light can get in or out.

Sadly, the harder we try to hold on to what we've got, the less able we are to do so. So we try still harder, which eventually drags us even deeper into the black hole of contraction. Are you like that? Do you know anybody who is?

Think of change as the movement between where we are and where we're not. That leaves only two directions for change: either moving forward or slipping backward. We either become more contracted or more expanded.

The next step is to link change to how we feel. If we feel afraid, change is dragging us backward. If we feel open, change is pushing us forward.

Change is not a thing-in-itself, but a movement of our consciousness. By tuning in, by paying attention, we get clues to the state of our being.

Change, then, is not an outcome or something to be acquired. Change is a shift of our consciousness, of our being, of our humanity, of our attention, of our relationship with all other beings in the universe.

We are either "more in relationship" or "less in relationship." Change is the movement in either of those directions. The exciting part is that we possess the ability to decide which way we go…and to know in the moment which way we're moving.

Closed, open; open, closed. Two directions in the universe. The choice is yours. Do you see the profound opportunity available to you? What an extraordinary way to live!

Enlightenment is not reserved for the sainted. Rather, it comes to us as we become more sensitive to ourselves. Eventually, we become our own guides, alerting ourselves to our state, moment by moment: *open…closed…open…closed.*

Listen to your inner voice, your ally, and feel what it's like to be open and closed. Experience the instant of choice in both directions. You will feel the awareness growing. It may be only a flash at first, so be alert. This feeling is accessible, but only if you avoid the black hole of contraction.

Are you afraid that you're totally contracted? Don't be—it's doubtful. The fact that you're still reading this book suggests that you're moving in the opposite direction. You're more like a running back seeking the open field. You can see the opportunity gleaming in the distance. In the open direction.

Understand that I'm not saying that change itself is a point on the path; rather, it's the all-important movement.

Change is *in you*, not *out there*.

What path are you on? The path of liberation? Or the path of crystallization?

As we know, change can be for the better or for the worse.

If change is happening *inside* of you, it is for the worse only if you remain closed to it. The key, then, is your attitude—your acceptance or rejection of change. Change can be for the better only if you accept it. And it will certainly be for the worse if you don't.

Remember, change is nothing in itself. Without you, change doesn't exist. Change is happening inside of each of us, giving us clues to where we are at any point in time.

Rejoice in change, for it's a sign you are alive.

Are we open? Are we closed? If we're open, good things are bound to happen. If we're closed, things will only get worse.

According to Golas, it's as simple as that. Whatever happens defines where we are. *How* we are is *where* we are. It cannot be any other way. For change is life.

Charles Darwin wrote, "It is not the strongest of the species that survive, nor the most intelligent, but the one that proves itself most responsive to change."

The growth of your business, then, is its change. Your role is to go with it, to be with it, to share the joy, embrace the opportunities, meet the challenges, learn the lessons.

Remember, there are three kinds of people: (1) those who make things happen; (2) those who let things happen; and (3) those who wonder what the hell happened. The people who make things happen are masters of change. The other two are its victims.

Which type are you?

The Big Change

If all this is going to mean anything to the life of your business, you have to know when you're going to leave it. At what point, in your business's rise from where it is now to where it can ultimately grow, are you going to sell it? Because if you don't have a clear picture of when you want out, your store is the master of your destiny, not the reverse.

As we stated earlier, the most valuable form of money is equity, and unless your business vision includes your equity and how you will use it to your advantage, you will forever be consumed by your business.

Your business is potentially the best friend you ever had. It is your business's nature to serve you, so let it. If, however, you are not a wise steward, if you do not tell your business what you expect from it, it will run rampant, abuse you, use you, and confuse you.

Change. Growth. Equity.

Focus on the point in the future when you will take leave of your business. Now reconsider your goals in that context. Be specific. Write them down.

Skipping this step is like tiptoeing through earthquake country. Who can say where the fault line is waiting? And who knows exactly when your whole world may come crashing down around you?

Former GE CEO Jack Welch famously said that we must all eat change for breakfast. From this day forward, don't skip your breakfast.

Which brings us to the subject of *time*. But first, let's listen to what John has to say about change. ✤

CHAPTER

20

YOU Can Control Your Change

John K. Rost

Change the changeable, accept the unchangeable, and remove yourself from the unacceptable.

—Denis Waitley

It's obvious to all of us that change is inevitable. What isn't so obvious is that there are five kinds of change:

- Change over which we have no control.
- Change we could control if we had the right resources.
- Change we can control.
- Change we allow.
- Change we create.

Let's look at them as they relate to your insurance store.

There are a number of examples of change you can't control: one of the insurance carriers for whom you write policies goes out of business; you lose the lease on your storefront and negotiation with the landlord simply isn't possible; your key agent decides to resign or retire and nothing you say or offer in terms of compensation will persuade that person otherwise; or you, as owner, become seriously ill, and are forced to leave your business. We really don't like to think about that last one, but events like that are a very real part of life.

Of course, there is also the kind of change we could control if we had all the resources we need at our disposal: you could buy the building that houses your business from the landlord; you could hire a better agent to replace the one you're losing; or you could find someone to run your business while you get treated for your illness…if you had the resources.

There is also change we can control: if the needs of your customer change, you can likely add provider companies that will meet those needs; if an agent or team member is not performing up to your expectations, you can replace that person; if you find that many of your customers prefer to come into your store during times not compatible with your hours of operation, you can change those hours.

Then, there is change we allow. Something "happens" to us or our store, and we say, "That's a good thing…I will decide to go along with it." (More on that soon.)

Finally, there is change we create: if you want more prospects, you can do more effective advertising or give "Max" more hours to stand in front of your store and draw in more people; if you want to grow your enterprise and ensure your retirement, you can open more stores; if you want to develop the skills that can help you reach your goals, you can find mentors and teachers to help you.

Very simply, my advice is to focus on those changes you can control and create, rather than dwelling on the things you can't control, or can't control because you are short on resources. You really CAN control your change!

Very honestly, I have occasionally been accused of resisting change. There have been many times when an owner will come to us and say, "I want to try this," or "I want to try that." While we welcome new ideas, we also know what has been tried before. As a result, we generally know what works and what doesn't. After all, we have a hundred stores, and years of experience, both in development and in daily operations.

But this is where "change we allow" comes into play. It's when someone sees something that could work better, or sees something completely new.

Recently, I visited a franchisee in Texas who had a banner out in front of the store that I had never seen before. It read, "Insure four cars for the price of one."

I asked, "What's that all about? How can you do that?"

Our owner responded, "We have insurance carriers in Texas that will do what's called a named operator insurance. So in other words, they're insuring you as a driver, and you can drive any of your four vehicles. What they're not doing is insuring your four vehicles all on the road at the same time."

I took a closer look at this, and it made perfect sense. Obviously, if the insured has three other drivers in the house, they had to be named, which would make the coverage more expensive. But if one driver has four or more cars, the rates will be based on the most expensive vehicle.

The store owner wanted to create an ad that sold that concept, knowing that some people who came in would not fit that under-writing requirement—but prospective customers would still come in.

I responded, "That's an interesting idea. We've never done anything like that before. Let's give it a shot."

So our graphic designer created artwork that employed our colors, our logo, and all of the necessary disclosures, and the plan was off and running, with my full support, as well as the support of our home office team.

In the final analysis, change is not something to fear. It's something to embrace. Even change that you initially see as negative can ultimately prove to be positive, and can make you and your enterprise better and more successful. Now let's see what Michael has to say about time. ❧

21

On the Subject of Time

Michael E. Gerber

Take time to deliberate; but when the time for action arrives, stop thinking and go in.

—Andrew Jackson

"I'm running out of time!" entrepreneurs often lament. "I've got to learn how to manage my time more carefully!"

Of course, they see no real solution to this problem. They're just worrying the subject to death. Singing the business-person's blues.

Some make a real effort to control time. Maybe they go to time management classes, or faithfully try to record their activities during every hour of the day.

But it's hopeless. Even when people work harder, even when they keep precise records of their time, there's always a shortage of it. It's as if they're looking at a square clock in a round universe. Something doesn't fit. The result: the entrepreneur is constantly chasing work, money, life. And as a country song once put it, "I'm always running…and always running behind."

The reason is simple. Owners don't see time for what it really is. They think of time with a small "t," rather than Time with a capital "T."

Yet Time is simply another word for *your life*. It's your ultimate asset, your gift at birth—and you can spend it any way you want. Do you know how you want to spend it? Do you have a plan?

How do *you* deal with Time? Are you even conscious of it? If you are, I bet you are constantly locked into either the future or the past. Relying on either memory or imagination.

Do you recognize these voices? "Once I get through this, I can have a drink/go on a vacation/retire." "I remember when I was young and selling insurance was satisfying."

As you go to bed at midnight, are you thinking about waking up at 6 a.m. so that you can get to the office by 7 a.m. so that you can be ready for customers by 8 a.m. so that you can go to lunch by noon, because you've got an appointment at 2 p.m. and two hours of record-keeping that needs to be finished by 5…?

Most of us are prisoners of the future or the past. While pinballing between the two, we miss the richest moments of our life—the present. Trapped forever in memory or imagination, we are strangers to the here and now. Our future is nothing more than an extension of our past, and the present is merely the background.

It's sobering to think that right now each of us is at a precise spot somewhere between the beginning of our Time (our birth) and the end of our Time (our death).

No wonder everyone frets about Time. What really terrifies us is that we're using up our life and we can't stop it.

It feels as if we're plummeting toward the end with nothing to break our free fall. Time is out of control! Understandably, this is horrifying, mostly because the real issue is not time with a small "t" but Death with a big "D."

From the depths of our existential anxiety, we try to put Time in a different perspective—all the while pretending we can manage it. We talk about Time as though it were something other than what it is. "Time is money," we announce, as though that explains it.

But what every entrepreneur should know is that Time is life. And Time ends! Life ends! The big, walloping, irresolvable problem is that we don't know how much Time we have left.

Do you feel that fear? Do you want to get over it? Let's look at Time more seriously.

To fully grasp Time with a capital "T", you have to ask the Big Question: *How do I wish to spend the rest of my Time?*

Because I can assure you that if you don't ask that Big Question with a big "Q," you will forever be assailed by the little questions. You'll shrink the whole of your life to *this time* and *next time* and the *last time*—all the while wondering, *What time is it?*

It's like running around the deck of a sinking ship worrying about where you left the keys to your cabin.

You must accept that you have only so much Time; that you're using up that Time second by precious second. And that your Time, your life, is the most valuable asset you have. Of course, you can use your Time any way you want. But unless you choose to use it as richly, as rewardingly, as excitingly, as intelligently, as *intentionally* as possible, you'll squander it and fail to appreciate it.

Indeed, if you are oblivious to the value of your Time, you'll commit the single greatest sin: You will live your life unconscious of its passing you by.

Until you deal with Time with a capital "T," you'll worry about time with a small "t" until you have no Time—or life—left. Then your Time will be history . . . along with your life.

Be vs. Do

Remember when we all asked, "What do I want to be when I grow up?" It was one of our biggest concerns as children.

136 *The E-Myth Insurance Store*

Notice that the question isn't: "What do I want to *do* when I grow up?" It's: "What do I want to *be?*"

Shakespeare wrote, "To be or not to be." Not, "To do or not to do."

But when you grow up, people always ask you, "What do you *do?*" How did the question change from *being* to *doing?* How did we miss the critical distinction between the two?

Even as children, we sensed the distinction. The real question we were asking was not what we would end up *doing* when we grew up, but who we would *be.*

We were talking about a *life* choice, not a *work* choice. We instinctively saw it as a matter of how we spend our Time, not what we do *in* time.

Look to children for guidance. I believe that as children we instinctively saw Time as life and tried to use it wisely. As children, we wanted to make a life choice, not a work choice. As children, we didn't know—or care—that work had to be done on time, on budget.

Until you see Time for what it really is—your life span—you will always ask the wrong question.

Until you embrace the whole of your Time and shape it accordingly, you will never be able to fully appreciate the moment.

Until you fully appreciate every second that comprises Time, you will never be sufficiently motivated to live those seconds fully.

Until you're sufficiently motivated to live those seconds fully, you will never see fit to change the way you are. You will never take the quality and sanctity of Time seriously.

And unless you take the sanctity of Time seriously, you will continue to struggle to catch up with something behind you. Your frustrations will mount as you try to snatch the second that just whisked by.

If you constantly fret about time with a small "t," then big-T Time will blow right past you. And you'll miss the whole point, the real truth about Time: You can't manage it; you never could. You can only *live* it.

And so that leaves you with these questions: How do I live my life? How do I give significance to it? How can I be here now, in this moment?

Once you begin to ask these questions, you'll find yourself moving toward a much fuller, richer life. But if you continue to be caught up in the banal work you do every day, you're never going to find the time to take a deep breath, exhale, and be present in the now.

So let's talk about the subject of *work*. But first, let's find out what John has to say about time. ✤

Your Goal Should be Freedom

John K. Rost

There is only one success—to be able to spend your life in your own way.
—Christopher Morley

Way back in 1964, the Rolling Stones had a hit (still playing on the radio today, as most of their venerable hits are) titled "Time Is On My Side." This song has nothing to do with insurance stores, but it has everything to do with my philosophy toward time.

We all have a limited number of minutes, hours, days, weeks, months, and years on this planet. We don't know how many we have, so we have to use them the best way we see fit.

Some people sleep them away. Some people drink them away. Some go to school forever. Some dream about things (or fear things) that may never happen. But, sadly, most people just work them away! "Tomorrow, and tomorrow, and tomorrow, creeps in this petty pace from day to day," said William Shakespeare.

Well, I believe that life should be anything but boring, anything but a petty pace, and anything but all work! Time should work for us, rather than the other way around. Time should be on our side!

The fact is, a successful insurance store—and a successful life—is all about managing choices, not managing time. Most of us never seem to have enough of our own time because of a lack of systems, and a shortage of personal discipline. We don't work effectively, and therefore we waste time.

To demonstrate this to yourself, make a list of the things you do in a typical day. I believe you will discover that your time is allocated among four kinds of activities:

- Those things you *have* to do;
- Those things you *want* to do;
- Those things *someone else* should be doing; and
- Those things *no one* should be doing.

Of course, you *have* to submit paperwork on new policies you write—or have someone on your team handle it in a timely and accurate manner. You *have* to pay the rent, do payroll, handle accounting, or have someone on your team do it. If you're one of our franchisees, you have to find someone to dress up in the Max costume to draw prospects into your store. You certainly don't want to put yourself or your agents into that costume. *Not* a good use of your time.

In the worst-case scenario, many owners are likely wasting time by being technicians. But the big advantage of growth is that it creates opportunities for others to become the masters of the technical jobs. You become the master of the system.

Long ago I decided that, as the CEO, I should not try to fulfill any job duty that was required daily in order for the business to function. I am no longer an insurance agent because I employed agents to do that job. I no longer make bank deposits and reconcile bank accounts. I no longer pay the bills or process payroll. Instead, I approve bills to be paid and approve the hiring of the staff we need.

Could I do this in the early days of my business? Of course not. But I worked on all of these areas with the idea of managing my time more effectively and growing the business. Look around at the business world. Is the CEO of Ford Motor Company building cars or making bank deposits? Why, then, should you, as the highest paid (if not now, at least eventually) member of your agency, be making bank deposits and buying office supplies for the store?

Technology offers you the option to do many vital things in a much shorter period of time. Make good use of technology. Open an online account with an office supply chain. Never purchase in person when you can save time by buying online and having things delivered. Don't waste time eating out each day if you are constantly swamped. Prepare lunch at home—as I still do most days—and eat in the office. You will save money and probably be healthier as a result. It will certainly save you time.

If you do not have the budget for a full-time bookkeeper you can hire one part-time. There are options available to you the business owner. Make it a goal to release certain functions of your agency as you hit certain levels. I can remember being the agent, accountant, human resource manager, and janitor, as well as buying supplies at the end of the day. That's what it takes in the beginning. Along the way, you find others to do these activities and give them the opportunity to learn, succeed, and fail. As a manager, I hope that the team I lead learns from both successes and failures.

For me personally, one of the greatest benefits of being the owner is having the ability to decide how I spend my time. When I ask new franchise owners what it is they hope to achieve by owning their business, it almost always comes down to having control over their time.

I am blessed to have witnessed numerous franchise owners explaining that they now have options that did not exist when they were working for others. The opportunity to coach a child in sports after school became possible. A single mother was able to drive her children to school and then pick them up in the afternoon. The owner has far more flexibility in taking advantage of a myriad of family opportunities—and handling times of crisis—than an employee. These stories only came true after the owner learned how to follow a system and then developed a team that was working in the business on behalf of the owner.

Take a look at the things you are doing daily and examine who else could handle those tasks. At what point in the growth of the business will you turn over these tasks? Hold yourself accountable for turning them over. Give your staff the opportunity to do significant things within your business (within certain limits, of course). You may find that, at times, others may actually perform certain functions better than you can. And by turning these things over, your time will be spent focused on the things you choose to do.

Michael asked the "Big Question:" *How do I wish to spend the rest of my Time?*

I told you at the very beginning of this book that I no longer write insurance policies. In fact, what I do is own insurance stores, and other people meet with clients and write policies. That means I can spend my time doing what I really want to do.

I take one week of vacation—alone, with my family, or with wonderful friends—every month of the year. That's twelve weeks, or three months of vacation annually. You can do that, too, if you establish your E-Myth systems and manage your time.

I have climbed the highest mountain—including Mt. Everest—on each of the seven continents. You may not want to do that (it's a LOT of hard work!) but you can determine what mountains you want to climb—and you can do it if you establish your E-Myth systems and manage your time.

Time really can be on your side. When you take control of your time, you will take control of your enterprise...and your life. You will enjoy freedom! Now let's see what Michael has to teach us about work. ❧

CHAPTER
23

On the Subject of Work

Michael E. Gerber

The man who has the largest capacity for work and thought is the man who is bound to succeed.

—Henry Ford

Perception is strong; sight is weak. In strategy it is important to see distant things as if they were close and to take a distanced view of close things.

In the business world, as the saying goes, the entrepreneur knows something about everything, the technician knows everything about something, and the switchboard operator just knows everything.

In an insurance business, owners/agents see their natural work as the work of the technician. The Supreme Technician. Often to the exclusion of everything else.

After all, agents get zero preparation working as a manager and spend no time thinking as an entrepreneur—those just aren't courses that have been offered to them. By the time they own their own insurance store, they're just doing it, doing it, doing it.

At the same time, they want everything—freedom, respect, money. Most of all, they want to rid themselves of meddling bosses and start their own business. That way they can be their own boss and take home all the money. These agents are in the throes of an entrepreneurial seizure.

Agents who have past success in writing policies for clients believe they have what it takes to run a business. It's not unlike the plumber who becomes a contractor because he's a great plumber. Sure, he may be a great plumber…but it doesn't necessarily follow that he knows how to build a business that does this work.

It's the same for an agent. So many of them are surprised to wake up one morning and discover that they're nowhere near as equipped for owning their own store as they thought they were.

More than any other subject, work is the cause of obsessive-compulsive behavior by many entrepreneurs.

Work. You've got to do it every single day.

Work. If you fall behind, you'll pay for it.

Work. There's either too much or not enough.

So many people describe work as what they do when they're busy. Some discriminate between the work they *could* be doing and the work they *should* be doing.

But according to the E-Myth, they're exactly the same thing. The work you *could* do and the work you *should* do are identical. Let me explain.

Strategic Work Versus Tactical Work

Insurance store owners can do only two kinds of work: strategic work and tactical work.

Tactical work is easier to understand, because it's what almost every owner/agent does almost every minute of every hour of every day. It's called getting the job done. It's called doing business.

Tactical work includes filing, billing, answering the telephone, going to the bank, seeing clients, and following through on cancellations.

The E-Myth says that tactical work is all the work owners find themselves doing in a business to *avoid* doing the strategic work.

"I'm too busy," most of them will tell you.

"How come nothing goes right unless I do it myself?" they complain in frustration.

Owners say these things when they're up to their ears in tactical work. But most of them don't understand that if they had done more strategic work, they would have less tactical work to do.

Owners are doing strategic work when they ask the following questions:

- Why am I in this business?
- What will my business look like when it's done?
- What must my business look, act, and feel like in order for it to compete successfully?
- What are the key indicators of my business?

Please note that I said owners *ask* these questions when they are doing strategic work. I didn't say these are the questions they necessarily answer.

That is the fundamental difference between strategic work and tactical work. Tactical work is all about *answers*: How to do this. How to do that.

Strategic work, in contrast, is all about *questions*: What business are we really in? Why are we in that business? Who specifically is our business determined to serve? When will I sell this business? How and where will this business be doing business when I sell it? And so forth.

Not that strategic questions don't have answers. Owners who commonly ask strategic questions know that once they ask such a question, they're already on their way to *envisioning* the answer. Question and answer are part of a whole. You can't find the right answer until you've asked the right question.

Tactical work is much easier, because the question is always more obvious. In fact, you don't ask the tactical question; instead, the question arises from a result you need to get or a problem you need to solve. Billing a client is tactical work. Submitting claims is tactical work. Firing an employee is tactical work. Seeing a client is tactical work.

Tactical work is the stuff you do every day in your business. Strategic work is the stuff you plan to do to create an exceptional store/business/enterprise.

In tactical work, the question comes from *out there* rather than *in here*. The tactical question is about something *outside* of you, whereas the strategic question is about something *inside* of you.

The tactical question is about something you need to do, whereas the strategic question is about something you want to do. Want vs. need.

If tactical work consumes you,

- you are always reacting to something outside of you;
- your store runs you; you don't run it;
- your employees run you; you don't run them; and
- your life runs you; you don't run your life.

You must understand that the more strategic work you do, the more intentional your decisions, your business, and your life become. *Intention* is the byword of strategic work.

Everything on the outside begins to serve you, to serve your vision, rather than forcing you to serve it. Everything you *need* to do is congruent with what you *want* to do. It means you have a vision, an aim, a purpose, a strategy, an *envisioned* result.

Strategic work is the work you do to *design* your business, to design your life. Tactical work is the work you do to *implement* the design created by strategic work.

Without strategic work, there is no design. Without strategic work, all that's left is keeping busy.

There's only one thing left to do. It's time to take action. But first, let's listen to what John has to say on the subject of work. ✤

Make "Work" Work for You

John K. Rost

Never work just for money or power. They won't save your soul or help you sleep at night.

—Marian Wright Edelman

I don't think there is any escaping the fact that if we own an insurance store— whether an independent store or a Fiesta Auto Insurance store, or group of stores—we will have to work. We will have to invest our time and expend our energy.

But one of the key principles of the E-Myth strategy for business and enterprise is that, by implementing the right processes and building on the right systems, the "work" piece of our lives should fall into place and be completely manageable. Enjoyable, even!

Yes, I admit I work hard. But I also play hard. I enjoy my work and I enjoy my play. And neither work nor play causes me much stress. Sure, the swings in the economy can be challenging, but my foundation is built on solid rock rather than shifting sand, so I move forward without fear. In short, I make "work" work for me.

Recently, I've been taking pictures on my iPhone of my computer on a desk. The desk is on the balcony of a resort. The balcony of the resort overlooks the Caribbean or the South Pacific. I text or email those photos to my superstar franchisees with a message that simply reads, "You should be here!" Some of them have already emailed photos of themselves in Hawaii or the Bahamas to me.

I'm not being mean! The truth is: I know they *will* be there—probably soon. They will be there because they are learning these three things about work, and about life:

- Stay on top of it.
- Get ahead of it.
- Anticipate the unexpected.

Work can become unmanageable if we don't stay on top of it. I have a friend (not in the insurance business) who hates working with numbers, so he falls behind on keeping the daily, weekly, and monthly records that he needs every year to complete and file his corporate taxes. When the tax deadline approaches, he files an extension. Then, a few days before the six-month extension expires, he scrambles to pull together his records and turn them over to his amazingly patient accountant. This causes considerable stress for both of them, and it distracts my friend from going about his normal and necessary business tasks.

I keep reminding him that his life would be more enjoyable if he kept on top of this essential task, but he simply counters with, "You *know* I hate numbers."

If you want your insurance store to create freedom in your life—if you want to make more time for yourself—it's not only important to stay on top of your work, it's also a great practice to get ahead of it. Control procrastination and you control stress. Control a bigger piece of your future on a day-to-day basis, and you will control your long-term future!

In terms of anticipating the unexpected, I'm not suggesting that you live in constant fear. I'm simply saying that when unpredictable things happen, know that they are a part of life, and you can deal with them. Don't let the unexpected sink your attitude—or your business.

When we examine the nature of the insurance agent's job, we see that it is basically the job of a technician. We perform certain tasks for each client by discussing their needs, quoting, selling, and servicing. It is a technician's job.

If Michael and I can convince you of anything, it is that you do not want to go through life as a technician. The good news is that you can find talented individuals who can learn how to accomplish these tasks and are quite happy and fulfilled doing the technician's job.

Since you have taken on the challenge of insurance store ownership (or are considering that right now), you are obviously up for the challenge. If, at any time in your career, "work" is not working as you would like, then change it. I express this attitude within our organization all the time. And that's also why Michael always stresses that the owner needs to develop strategic thinking.

Why is something being done in a certain way? What do we hope to accomplish? Why isn't it working? And when it isn't working, where do we turn to find a solution?

I am constantly in search of solutions…often when there isn't really a problem. That's because I know things can always be done better.

Most people, when they face a challenge, accept the situation and see it as an event over which they have no control. If the business just isn't growing anymore, they blame the economy, competition, poor staffing, or a hundred other factors—real or imaginary. But excuses aren't going to get you moving. As the owner, it is your job to become the strategic thinker in order to work through these challenges.

Work will seem a lot less like work when you get on top of it, get ahead of it, and learn to deal with the unexpected. Let's see what Michael has to say about taking action. ❧

CHAPTER
25

On the Subject of
Taking Action

Michael E. Gerber

Deliberation is the work of many men. Action, of one alone.
                                              —Charles de Gaulle

I t's time to get started, time to take action. Time to stop thinking about the old ways and start thinking about the new way. It's not a matter of coming up with better practices; it's about reinventing the ways of the insurance store.

And the owner has to take personal responsibility for it.

That means owners have to be interested. They cannot abdicate accountability for the business on insurance, the administration of the store, or the finances of the store.

Although the goal is to create systems into which owners can plug reasonably competent people—systems that allow the business to run without them—owners must take responsibility for that happening.

I can hear the chorus: "But we're insurance agents. We shouldn't have to know about this. It's beneath us." And to that I say: Of course you should!

All too often, as we've discussed, owners take no responsibility for the business, but instead delegate tasks without any understanding of what it takes to do them; without any interest in what their people are actually doing; without any sense of what it feels like to be at the front desk when a client comes in and has to wait for 45 minutes; and without any appreciation for the entity that is creating their livelihood.

Owners can open the portals of change in an instant. All you have to do is say, "I don't want to do it that way anymore." Saying it will begin to set you free—even though you don't yet understand what the business will look like after it's been reinvented.

This demands an intentional leap from the known into the unknown. It further demands that you live there—in the unknown—for a while. It means discarding the past, everything you once believed to be true.

Think of it as soaring rather than plunging.

Thought Control

You should now be clear about the need to organize your thoughts first, then your business. Because the organization of your thoughts is the foundation for the organization of your business.

If we try to organize our business without organizing our thoughts, we will fail to attack the problem.

We have seen that organization is not simply time management. Nor is it people management. Nor is it tidying up desks or alphabetizing client files. Organization is first, last, and always cleaning up the mess of our minds.

By learning how to *think* about the business, by learning how to *think* about our priorities, and by learning how to *think* about our lives, we prepare ourselves to do righteous battle with the forces of failure.

Right thinking leads to right action—and now is the time to take action. Because it is only through action that we can translate thoughts into movement in the real world, and, in the process, find fulfillment.

So, first we ***think*** about what we want to do. Then we must *do* it. Only in this way will we be fulfilled.

How do you put the principles we've discussed in this book to work in your insurance store? To find out, accompany me down the path once more:

1. ***Create a story about your business.*** Your story should be an idealized version of your store, a vision of what the preeminent business in your field should be and why. Your story must become the very heart of your operation. It must become the spirit that mobilizes it, as well as everyone who walks through the doors. Without this story, your business will be reduced to plain work.

2. ***Organize your business so that it breathes life into your story.*** Unless your business can faithfully replicate your story in action, it all becomes fiction. In that case, you'd be better off not telling your story at all. And without a story, you'd be better off leaving your business the way it is and just hoping for the best.

Here are some tips for organizing your insurance business:

- Identify the key functions of your business.
- Identify the essential processes that link those functions.
- Identify the results you have determined your store will produce.
- Clearly state in writing how each phase will work.

Take it step by step. Think of your business as a program, a piece of software, a system. It is a collaboration, a collection of processes dynamically interacting with one another.

Of course, your business is also people.

3. ***Engage your people in the process. Why is this the third*** step rather than the first? Because, contrary to the advice most business experts will give you, you must never engage your people in the process until you yourself are clear about what you intend to do.

The need for consensus is a disease of today's addled mind. It's a product of our troubled and confused times. When people don't know what to believe in, they often ask others to tell them. To ask is not to lead, but to follow.

The prerequisite of sound leadership is first to know where you wish to go.

And so, "What do *I* want?" becomes the first question; not, "What do *they* want?" In your own business, the vision must first be yours. To follow another's vision is to abdicate your personal accountability, your leadership role, your true power.

In short, the role of leader cannot be delegated or shared. And without leadership, no insurance store will ever succeed.

Despite what you have been told, *win-win* is a secondary step, not a primary one. The opposite of *win-win* is not necessarily *"they lose."*

Let's say "they" can win by choosing a good horse. The best choice will not be made by consensus. "Guys, which horse do you think we should ride?" will always lead to endless and worthless discussions. By the time you're done jawing, the horse will have already left the post.

Before you talk to your people about what you intend to do in your business and why you intend to do it, you need to reach an agreement with yourself.

It's important to know: (1) *exactly* what you want, (2) how you intend to proceed, (3) what's important to you and what isn't, and, (4) what you want the business to be and how you want it to get there.

Once you have that agreement, it's critical that you engage your people in a discussion about what you intend to do and why. Be clear—both with yourself and with them.

The Story

The story is paramount because it is your vision. Tell it with passion and conviction. Tell it with precision. Never hurry a great story. Unveil it slowly. Don't mumble or show embarrassment. Never apologize or display false modesty. Look your audience in the eyes and tell your story as though it is the most important one they'll ever hear about business. Your business. The business into which you intend to pour your heart, your soul, your intelligence, your imagination, your time, your money, and your sweaty persistence.

Get into the storytelling zone. Behave as though it means everything to you. Show no equivocation when telling your story.

These tips are important because you're going to tell your story over and over—to clients, to new and old employees, and to your family and friends. You're going to tell it at your church or synagogue; to your card-playing or fishing buddies; and to organizations such as Kiwanis, Rotary, YMCA, Hadassah, and Boy Scouts.

There are few moments in your life when telling a great story about a great business is inappropriate.

If it is to be persuasive, you must love your story. Do you think Walt Disney loved his Disneyland story? Or Ray Kroc, his McDonald's story? What about Dave Smith at Federal Express? Or Debbie Fields at Mrs. Field's Cookies? Or Tom Watson, Jr., at IBM?

Do you think these people loved their stories? Do you think others loved (and still love) to hear them? I daresay *all* successful entrepreneurs have loved the story of their business. Because that's what true entrepreneurs do: they tell stories that come to life in the form of their business.

Remember: a great story never fails. A great story is always a joy to hear.

In summary, you first need to clarify, both for yourself and for your people, the *story* of your business. Then you need to detail the *process* your business must go through to make your story become reality.

I call this the business development process. Others call it reengineering, continuous improvement, reinventing your business, or total quality management.

Whatever you call it, you must take three distinct steps to succeed:

- *Innovation.* Continue to find better ways of doing what you do.

- *Quantification.* Once that is achieved, quantify the impact of these improvements on your business.

- *Orchestration.* Once these improvements are verified, orchestrate this better way of running your business so that it becomes your standard, to be repeated time and again.

In this way, the system works—no matter who's using it. And you've built an insurance business that works consistently, predictably, systematically. A business you can depend on to operate exactly as promised, every single time.

Your vision, your people, your process—all linked.

A superior business is a creation of your imagination, a product of your mind. So fire it up and get started!

I hope you agree with me...so that now you can take action.

And now, I'm sure, you will. Here are John's parting words about taking action. ❧

26

Act on Your Dreams

John K. Rost

You don't have to be great to get started, but you have to get started to be great.

—Les Brown

The motto of my company, Fiesta Auto Insurance/Fiesta Tax Services, is very simply, "Dream, Believe, Achieve

To me, "Dream" means to have a vision of what you want to be and where you want your life to go. Do you want to escape the limits on your life that you now know?

"Believe" means that you fully know that you can bring all the elements of success together—the people, procedures, products, and places, and then apply the systems that make it all work. If you do need help, you know where to go to get it, and you aren't afraid to ask for it.

"Achieve" means your business—your insurance store—works for you, rather than the other way around. It means you have the opportunity to actually live the dream you created in your mind.

Michael advises you to "create a story about your business." I couldn't agree more.

My company began as my personal dream. I wanted to work for myself, rather than for someone else. But, more important than that, I did not want to be a technician...doing the same thing every day to make a handful of dollars. I wanted to own my business, rather than the business owning me. That's why Michael's E-Myth principles became so crucial to the development of my business. I recognized that "systems" really were the answer.

Michael also made it easy for me to *believe*, because I could readily see that what he teaches makes complete sense. As a result, I began to believe that an insurance store—especially a Fiesta Auto Insurance store—would be a great concept to franchise because it would meet the insurance needs of a huge segment of the population at competitive rates, it would be very consumer friendly, and it would ultimately make owners successful. It would be a turnkey business for its owners.

In reality it takes belief to make an owner truly successful. Yes, it all starts with hard work...some long hours and the support of family—"every business is a family business"—and an initial investment. But it is my belief in our franchise owners that empowers them to believe. We provide training, marketing support, and day-to-day involvement to guarantee that they are never alone. We want our owners to succeed beyond even their wildest dreams. I'm talking to *YOU* right now! I want you to become the owner of an E-Myth insurance store—whether one of our franchises or an independent store of your own—and *achieve!*

What can you achieve?

One of the biggest and most satisfying achievements that owners of an E-Myth insurance store ultimately experience is the sale of that store—and the comfortable (and possibly, early) retirement that the growth in equity provides. Imagine, for example, owning three insurance stores and selling them for $2 million each at the age of 45! I've seen owners actually do this. Because they worked *on* their businesses rather than *in* their businesses, they were able to apply the principles in this book, follow their dreams, believe in those very clear dreams, and achieve the comfortable standard of living that was the envy of their friends.

This really *can* be your life! It's time for you to start dreaming… and believing! It's time for you to take action!

To your success! ❧

AFTERWORD

Michael E. Gerber

For more than three decades, I've applied the E-Myth principles I've shared with you in this book to the successful development of thousands of small businesses throughout the world. Many have been independent insurance agents, as well as the owner/operators of insurance stores.

Few rewards are greater than seeing these E-Myth principles improve the work and lives of so many people. Those rewards include seeing these changes:

- Lack of clarity—clarified.
- Lack of organization—organized.
- Lack of direction—shaped into a path that is clearly, lovingly, passionately pursued.
- Lack of money or money poorly managed—money understood instead of coveted; created instead of chased; wisely spent or invested instead of squandered.
- Lack of committed people—transformed into a cohesive community working in harmony toward a common goal; discovering one another and themselves in the process; all the while expanding their understanding, their know-how, their interest, their attention.

After working with so many insurance professionals, I know that their companies can be much more than what most of them become. I also know that there is nothing preventing you from making your

insurance business all that it can be. It takes only desire and perseverance—coupled with the consistent application of E-Myth
principles—to see it through.

In this book—another in the E-Myth Expert series—the E-Myth
principles have been complemented and enriched by stories from John,
a real-life insurance master who has put these precepts to effective use
in his own company. John had the desire and perseverance to achieve
success beyond his wildest dreams. Now you can join him.

I hope this book has helped you clear your vision and set your
sights on a very bright future.

To your company!

———

ABOUT THE AUTHOR

Michael E. Gerber

Michael E. Gerber is the legend behind the E-Myth series of books, which includes *The E-Myth Revisited, E-Myth Mastery, The E-Myth Manager, The E-Myth Enterprise*, and *Awakening the Entrepreneur Within*. Collectively, his books have sold millions of copies worldwide. He is the founder of In the Dreaming Room™, a 2½-day process to awaken the entrepreneur within, and Origination, which trains facilitators to assist entrepreneurs in growing "turnkey" businesses. He is chairman of the Michael E. Gerber Companies. A highly sought-after speaker and consultant, he has trained hundreds of thousands of business owners in his career. Michael lives with his wife, Luz Delia, in Carlsbad, California.

ABOUT THE CO-AUTHOR

John K. Rost

John K. Rost is the President and founder of Fiesta Insurance Franchise Corporation (FIFC). FIFC is the franchisor for the Fiesta Auto Insurance and Tax Service franchise system. Fiesta Auto Insurance was founded in 2006 when Mr. Rost franchised his system, making it available in California and then nationwide. Currently stores have been opened in sixteen states, with a goal of having over 2,500 open by 2019.

Mr. Rost has been involved in the insurance industry since 1994, first as an employee, and then as the Founder and President of National Insurance Centers, a chain that he sold in 1998. It is currently active in a number of states.

Mr. Rost is not an insurance agent. In fact he has never written an insurance policy since Fiesta Auto Insurance was opened in January of 1999. He has a proven system to manage and grow an agency by working on the business and not in it. With his system working proficiently, he was able to invest his time pursuing additional goals and accomplishments.

In 2003 and 2004, Mr. Rost (also known as Adventure Guy) reached the summit of the highest mountains on all seven continents—including Mount Everest. He was the thirty-fifth American and ninety-sixth individual in the world to complete "The Seven Summits."

In his continued pursuit of challenges, he personally built an experimental airplane in his garage, affixing the wings after he transported his project to a nearby airport. He performed all of the test flying necessary to have the aircraft approved for flight throughout the United States, as well as internationally. Later he set two national and world speed records in this aircraft.

Mr. Rost currently lives in Huntington Beach, California, near the beach with his three college and high school-age children, Alec, Chris, and Emily. He enjoys a very active lifestyle and includes kiteboarding in most of his vacations.

His life is a validation of his business system: Dream, Believe, Achieve.

ABOUT THE SERIES

The E-Myth Expert series brings Michael E. Gerber's proven E-Myth philosophy to a wide variety of different professional business areas. The E-Myth, short for "Entrepreneurial Myth," is simple: Too many small businesses fail to grow because their leaders think like technicians, not entrepreneurs. Gerber's approach gives small enterprise leaders practical, proven methods that have already helped transform tens of thousands of businesses. Let the E-Myth Expert series boost your professional business today!

Books in the series include:
The E-Myth Attorney
The E-Myth Accountant
The E-Myth Optometrist
The E-Myth Chiropractor
The E-Myth Financial Advisor
The E-Myth Landscape Contractor
The E-Myth Architect
The E-Myth Real Estate Brokerage
The E-Myth Insurance Store

Forthcoming books in the series include:
The E-Myth Real Estate Investor
The E-Myth Dentist
The E-Myth Nutritionist
. . . and more than 300 other industries and professions

Learn more at: www.michaelegerber.com/co-author

Have you created an E-Myth enterprise? Would you like to become a co-author of an E-Myth book in your industry? Go to www.michaelegerber.com/co-author.

THE MICHAEL E. GERBER
ENTREPRENEUR'S LIBRARY
It Keeps Growing...

Thank you for reading another E-Myth Vertical book.

Who do you know who is an expert in their industry?

Who has applied the E-Myth to the improvement of their business as John K. Rost has?

Who can add immense value to others in his or her industry by sharing what he or she has learned?

Please share this book with that individual and share that individual with us.

❖

We at Michael E. Gerber Companies are determined to transform the state of small business and entrepreneurship worldwide. *You can help.*

To find out more, email us at Michael E. Gerber Partners, at Gerber@michaelegerber.com.

To find out how YOU can apply the E-Myth to YOUR practice, contact us at Gerber@michaelegerber.com.

Thank you for living your Dream, and changing the world.

MICHAEL E.GERBER
PARTNERS
Authors of Business Design

Michael E. Gerber, Co-Founder/Chairman
Michael E. Gerber Companies™
Creator of The E-Myth Evolution™
P.O. Box 131195, Carlsbad, CA 92013
760-752-1812 O • 760-752-9926 F
Gerber@michaelegerber.com
www.michaelegerber.com/are-you-the-one

Join The Evolution^{SM}

Attend the Dreaming Room Trainings
www.michaelegerber.com/dreaming-room

Awaken the Entrepreneur Within You
www.michaelegerber.com/facilitator-training

Michael E. Gerber Partners
www.michaelegerber.com/are-you-the-one

Listen to the Michael E. Gerber Radio Show
www.blogtalkradio.com/michaelegerber

Watch the latest videos
www.youtube.com/michaelegerber

Connect on LinkedIn
www.linkedin.com/in/michaelegerber

Connect on Facebook
www.facebook.com/MichaelEGerberCo

Follow on Twitter
http://twitter.com/michaelegerber

www.ingramcontent.com/pod-product-compliance
Lightning Source LLC
Chambersburg PA
CBHW031359180326
41458CB00043B/6542/J